Faith in the Age of Algorithms

Faith in the Age of Algorithms

When Machines Challenge Belief

Mira Qadari

Mindful Pages

Published in 2026

ISBN: 9789375361435 (PB)
ISBN: 9789375362876 (eBook)

Published by

Mindful Pages
Imprint of Alpha Editions LLC
312 W. 2nd St #1834
Casper, WY 82601, USA

Content

Introduction

On a winter evening, a driver follows the blue line on a navigation screen through a village she has never visited. The app insists on a narrow lane rather than the main road. An older man, standing by the post office, shakes his head and gestures otherwise. She hesitates for a moment, then trusts the glowing arrow and turns away from him. Somewhere else, a teenager scrolls through a feed that seems uncannily attuned to a private restlessness she has never voiced aloud. Elsewhere still, a quiet score—calculated from fragments of past behaviour—tips the balance between trust and suspicion, opening a door for one person while closing it for another. None of these moments announce themselves as moral crossroads. They arrive as conveniences, as efficiencies, as neutral aids to living well. Yet taken together they sketch a new condition of life: one in which judgement is increasingly delegated, anticipation automated, and the future pre-emptively shaped by systems that learn us faster than we learn ourselves.

At first glance, this appears to be a story about technology. It is not. It is a story about authority, agency, and meaning. It is about how human beings orient themselves when guidance comes not from elders, scriptures, or shared customs, but from predictive systems whose operations are largely invisible and whose confidence is expressed in numbers rather than words. The paradox at the heart of our moment is not that machines now calculate so much, but that as they do, the older language of calling, grace, conscience, and freedom has not vanished. It persists, sometimes stubbornly, sometimes awkwardly, often without clear footing. We still speak of being led, of surrendering what we cannot control, of acting responsibly even when outcomes are uncertain. We still pray, even as predictions proliferate. The question this book asks is simple to state and difficult to answer: when machines seem to know us so well, why do we continue to insist that our lives are more than the sum of their forecasts?

Prediction has always been a human obsession. Long before code, there were stars, entrails, lots, and omens. Societies devised elaborate ways to read the future not because they believed it was fixed, but because uncertainty was unbearable without shared rituals for facing it. What is new is not the desire to foresee, but the intimacy and scale of contemporary prediction. Algorithms do not merely speculate about weather or harvests; they insinuate themselves into friendship, romance, work, worship, and risk. They recommend what we should read, watch, buy, and believe. They rank us, sort us, and quietly decide how much friction we will encounter as we move through the world. They do this with an air of objectivity that previous forms of guidance rarely claimed. A priest might speak of discernment, a philosopher of prudence, a parent of wisdom earned through experience. An algorithm offers a score.

This shift has consequences that extend beyond convenience. When guidance arrives as a probability rather than a counsel, responsibility subtly changes shape. If an outcome was highly likely, how accountable was I for choosing otherwise? If a system warned me of risk, did I sin by ignoring it, or by obeying it too readily? If a recommendation anticipated my desire before I named it, was it revealing something true about me, or was it quietly training me to want what it could most easily supply? These questions are not abstract. They surface in everyday decisions about health, finance, relationships, and belief. They also surface in moments of moral unease, when compliance with a system feels easier than reflection, and dissent feels foolish in the face of data.

Faith traditions have long grappled with similar tensions. They have wrestled with the relationship between providence and freedom, between being known and being coerced, between trust and abdication. They have developed practices designed to slow decision-making, to thicken responsibility, and to hold individuals within communities of counsel and care. None of this history maps neatly onto contemporary technology. Algorithms are not gods, and data is not destiny. Yet the resonance is close enough to be unsettling. When people speak of "what the numbers say" with a reverence once reserved for sacred texts, something significant has shifted in the hierarchy of trust. When leaders defer to dashboards more readily than to testimony, authority has been reconfigured. When individuals outsource difficult judgements to systems that promise neutrality, conscience risks atrophy.

The central purpose of this book is not to lament these changes, nor to celebrate them. It is to offer a language for noticing what is happening, and a framework for responding without panic or complacency. The aim is neither conversion nor critique for its own sake, but literacy—moral, spiritual, and civic literacy—about the systems that increasingly mediate our lives. This requires demystifying how algorithms work, without collapsing into technical bravado. It also requires taking faith seriously, not as a private preference or a relic of the past, but as a set of practices and concepts forged precisely to address uncertainty, power, and human limitation.

One recurring image will frame this exploration: that of invisible weather. Algorithmic systems are like atmospheric conditions we live within rather than tools we consciously wield. They shape what feels normal, what seems possible, and what appears risky. Like weather, they are the result of many interacting forces. Like weather, they are often noticed only when they become extreme. And like weather, they invite both preparation and humility. We cannot control the climate of our digital environments alone, but we can learn to read the signs, to build shelters where needed, and to resist the fantasy that prediction equals mastery.

The chapters that follow move deliberately between experience, history, and practice. They begin with how code comes to feel like destiny, scripting days so quietly that its influence is mistaken for fate. They then turn back to older stories of providence and freedom, not to mine them for answers, but to recover a sense of proportion. Inside the so-called black box, we examine how data becomes judgement, and how feedback loops can harden possibility into probability. From there, attention shifts to the personalised self, sculpted by clicks and swipes, feeling both intimately known and perpetually observed. Prediction and risk are considered not only as technical achievements, but as moral postures that reshape our relationship to uncertainty and surrender.

Authority, too, demands reconsideration. When numbers sound more honest than people, when metrics outpace testimony, leadership itself is transformed. Communities—religious and otherwise—are being rewired by platforms that reward attention over fidelity and outrage over patience. Conscience is being formed in a scored world, where worthiness is tracked and comparison is constant. Practices of faith are migrating online, mediated by apps and streaks that both support and distort devotion. Finally, the book turns toward design, asking what it would mean to build systems that are humane, transparent, and accountable, and to accept shared responsibility for the worlds we are co-authoring.

Throughout, the goal is not to resolve theological debates or to issue policy prescriptions. It is to keep certain questions alive in a culture that prefers answers it can automate. What does it mean to act freely when probabilities press in from all sides? How do we remain responsible without pretending to be sovereign? Where should trust ultimately rest when expertise is distributed and authorship diffuse? And how might faith—understood broadly as a way of orienting life toward meaning beyond calculation—offer resources for living well amid predictive power?

The urgency of these questions is obvious. Decisions once made slowly and locally are now made instantly and at scale. Errors propagate faster than reflection. Yet the stakes are also timeless. Human beings have always sought signs that their lives are intelligible, that their choices matter, and that they are not alone in facing uncertainty. Algorithms intensify these desires rather than replacing them. They promise clarity, but often deliver new forms of dependence. They offer foresight, but sometimes erode wisdom. The challenge is not to reject them, but to refuse their quiet redefinition of what it means to be human.

This book is an invitation to stand at the intersection of faith and code without rushing to judgement. It assumes readers who are curious rather than defensive, sceptical without being cynical, and willing to examine their own habits of trust. It offers no nostalgia for a pre-digital past and no optimism that technology will save us from ourselves. Instead, it proposes that living thoughtfully in the age of algorithms requires practices of attention, humility, and courage—virtues as old as any tradition, newly tested by machines that never sleep.

The pages ahead will ask readers to notice when they treat systems as oracles, when they surrender judgement too quickly, and when they resist guidance out of misplaced pride. They will suggest ways of holding prediction lightly, of designing and choosing tools with care, and of recovering spaces for surprise and grace. The tension that animates this inquiry remains unresolved, and deliberately so. If machines can anticipate so much, what remains uncalculable about human life? If risk can be scored, what becomes of responsibility? And if guidance increasingly arrives in the language of probability, how might prayer, discernment, and freedom be reimagined rather than abandoned? The answers will not be delivered by any system. They will have to be practised.

Chapter 1
When Code Feels Like Destiny

The message arrives without drama. A recommendation appears on a screen at the edge of the day: a course to enrol in, a video to watch next, a job to consider, a person to follow. It does not claim authority. It does not demand obedience. It simply suggests. Yet later, when the path of a life is traced backward, that suggestion acquires a strange weight. The choice that followed feels less like a decision than a nudge, less like intention than inevitability. Many people can point to such moments now, when a quiet prompt seemed to know something they did not yet know themselves.

For most of human history, destiny was spoken of in mythic tones. It belonged to gods, stars, or inscrutable forces that lay beyond calculation. Fate descended from above; providence unfolded according to a will that could be trusted or resisted, but never audited. Today, destiny wears a different costume. It is expressed in charts and scores, probabilities and rankings. It arrives through interfaces designed to feel neutral, even helpful. The language has changed, but the sensation is familiar. Something unseen is shaping the field of possible actions, and the individual stands within it, wondering how much freedom remains.

This chapter begins with that sensation. Not with theory, but with the lived experience of being guided by systems that rarely announce themselves as guides. Algorithms quietly script our days, deciding which routes feel sensible, which voices sound credible, which futures appear realistic. We still speak of luck, chance, and calling, but those words now coexist with dashboards and data streams that claim a more precise grasp of how the world works. The first task is to name this shift for what it is: the emergence of code as a new language of fate.

The word *fate* once referred to a story told about the future after the fact. It was a way of making sense of what had already happened, of stitching coherence into suffering or success. Algorithms invert that relationship. They tell stories about the future in advance, then help to bring those stories about. A recommendation engine does not merely predict what someone might like; it actively shapes the conditions under which liking occurs. A navigation system does not simply describe traffic; it redistributes it. In these moments, prediction becomes participation. The future is no longer awaited so much as pre-arranged.

Consider a simple case. A music streaming service suggests a playlist tailored to a listener's recent habits. She accepts, discovering an artist she had never sought out. The songs become a soundtrack to a particular season of life. Months later, asked how she came to love that music, she might speak of taste, of coincidence, of being in the right mood at the right time. Rarely does she speak of the system that noticed a pattern and acted upon it. Yet without that intervention, the path of preference would have been different. Multiply this logic across careers, relationships, beliefs, and risks, and the stakes become clearer. The systems that learn from us also learn *us*.

To see why this matters, we need to pause and look more closely at what algorithms actually are. They are not oracles, and they are not minds. At their core, they are sets of instructions for identifying patterns in data and using those patterns to make predictions or decisions. They sort, rank, and optimise according to goals defined by human beings. A recommendation algorithm on a streaming platform, for example, analyses past behaviour—what was watched, for how long, at what time of day—and compares it with the behaviour of others deemed similar. From this, it infers what is likely to keep a viewer engaged next.

This process sounds technical, but its implications are profoundly human. Every step involves judgement. Which behaviours count as signals? Which similarities matter? What does "success" mean: time spent, satisfaction reported, subscriptions retained? These choices encode values, even when they are framed as neutral optimisation problems. By demystifying algorithms, we do not diminish their power; we clarify it. We see that they are not autonomous forces descending upon society, but artefacts shaped by incentives, assumptions, and trade-offs. The danger lies not in their complexity, but in the ease with which that complexity invites abdication.

Most people do not experience algorithms as tools they actively use. They experience them as conditions they inhabit. This is where the metaphor of invisible weather becomes useful. Like weather, algorithmic systems are pervasive and largely taken for granted. They influence mood, movement, and possibility without requiring constant attention. One does not wake each morning to negotiate with the atmosphere; one simply dresses accordingly and steps outside. In much the same way, people adapt to feeds, rankings, and defaults, allowing them to set the tone of days and the limits of expectation.

Habituation dulls agency. When a social media feed reliably supplies content that aligns with existing views, curiosity atrophies. When defaults are rarely changed, they come to feel like natural laws rather than design decisions. Over time, passivity grows not because people have chosen it, but because resistance requires effort that the system subtly discourages. The feed refreshes itself. The next video auto-plays. The path of least resistance becomes the path of greatest reinforcement. What begins as convenience hardens into custom.

This dynamic is not new, but its scale is unprecedented. Earlier forms of guidance—custom, tradition, authority—were mediated through relationships that allowed for negotiation and dissent. One could argue with an elder, reinterpret a text, or leave a community. Algorithmic guidance is more diffuse. It rarely confronts; it surrounds. Its influence is felt not as command, but as atmosphere. This makes it harder to resist and easier to internalise. People begin to anticipate what the system will reward and adjust themselves accordingly, often without conscious awareness.

At this point, the chapter turns toward its most unsettling question. When machines seem to know us better than we know ourselves, what happens to faith and freedom? Knowledge has always carried authority. To be known is to be vulnerable. Religious traditions have wrestled with this for centuries, offering images of a divine gaze that sees the heart without coercing the will. The claim was never that being known erased freedom, but that it made responsibility unavoidable. Algorithmic knowing feels different. It is partial, probabilistic, and relentlessly instrumental. Yet it often feels more immediate, more actionable, than older forms of judgement.

The temptation is to treat these systems as oracles. Not because they are wise, but because they are confident. They speak in the language of likelihood, which carries a persuasive force of its own. If something is highly probable, it begins to feel permissible. If a risk is quantified, it feels manageable. In this way, probability slides quietly into destiny. The future appears already written, and the role of the individual is reduced to compliance or error.

This chapter does not resolve that tension. It maps it. The pages ahead will move from the felt experience of algorithmic guidance to its underlying mechanics, then back out to its moral and spiritual implications. Readers will be invited to notice where they already defer to systems without reflection, where they resist them out of fear, and where a more thoughtful engagement might be possible. A short exercise at the chapter's end will ask not for answers, but for attention: to recall a recent moment when a system seemed to speak with authority, and to ask what was gained, and what was quietly surrendered.

The promise of this chapter is modest and demanding. It does not offer escape from algorithmic life, nor does it propose a return to some imagined past of unmediated freedom. Instead, it insists that understanding precedes judgement, and that literacy is a form of agency. To recognise when code feels like destiny is the first step toward refusing that feeling's inevitability. The weather may be invisible, but it is not unknowable. And once it is named, it can be met with something more than resignation.

Code as a New Language of Fate

On 6 September 2006, in Cambridge, Massachusetts, Facebook switched on a feature called the News Feed. Mark Zuckerberg announced it as a way to help users "stay connected" by automatically curating updates from friends. The reaction was swift and hostile. Thousands protested. Groups formed demanding its removal. What unsettled users was not surveillance in the legal sense—much of the information was already public—but the sensation of being arranged. The platform had begun to decide, moment by moment, what mattered most. Within weeks, the protests subsided. The feed stayed. A decade later, few could imagine the service without it.

Five words matter here. *The feed stayed.* What had felt intrusive came to feel inevitable. A design choice hardened into background reality. This is how fate begins to speak in code.

Algorithms now decide which headlines greet us in the morning, which route seems sensible on the way to work, which faces appear plausible as friends or partners, which applications are filtered out before a human ever sees them. These systems rarely issue commands. They offer likelihoods. They rank. They recommend. The effect, however, is cumulative. Over time, probability acquires the texture of destiny. The future feels pre-shaped, not imposed from above but assembled quietly, one optimisation at a time.

Older languages of fate were explicit about their sources. In Homer's epics, destiny belonged to the Moirai, who spun and cut the thread of life. In Christian theology, providence named a trust that events, however opaque, unfolded within divine care. Even when contested, these frameworks acknowledged their metaphysical claims. They located authority outside human systems. Code does something subtler. It presents itself as immanent, empirical, and corrective. Fate is no longer announced by oracles or priests but inferred from behaviour, displayed on dashboards, and updated in real time.

To see how this works, consider a story that has become commonplace. In 2014, Netflix publicly described how its recommendation algorithms influenced viewing choices at scale, noting that over 75 per cent of what users watched came from recommendations rather than searches (Netflix, 2014). For an individual viewer, the experience is banal. A series appears. It auto-plays. An evening passes. Yet when careers in writing rooms, commissioning budgets, and cultural conversations are traced backward, that nudge matters. A system designed to maximise retention reshapes taste. Taste reshapes production. Production reshapes what feels culturally available. Show, then name, then explain: a recommendation becomes a habit; the habit becomes a market signal; the signal becomes an industry constraint. The implication is not conspiracy but consequence.

Algorithms, stripped of mystique, are pattern-seeking machines. They measure past behaviour, compare it with other datasets, and generate predictions optimised for a goal. The goal may be engagement, efficiency, safety, or profit. Human judgement enters at every stage. Someone decides what counts as relevant data, how it is weighted, and which outcomes matter. A navigation app such as Google Maps, which expanded rapidly after Google acquired Waze in 2013, does not merely find the shortest route. It optimises for speed based on aggregated movement. When thousands follow the same advice, traffic itself changes. Residents of once-quiet streets in cities such as Los Angeles noticed this effect by 2017, as reported by the *Los Angeles Times*. The map redrew the neighbourhood.

Here the metaphor of fate sharpens. Traditional accounts of destiny grappled with the tension between foreknowledge and freedom. If the gods knew the outcome, were human choices meaningful? Algorithmic systems pose a different version of the problem. They do not know the future; they help produce it. A risk score used in lending does not predict default in the abstract. It influences who receives credit, which influences economic behaviour, which then feeds back into the data. Prediction becomes self-reinforcing. The weather vane begins to steer the wind.

Yet most people do not experience this as coercion. They experience it as convenience. The dashboard feels informative, not directive. When a fitness app reports a missed target, it appears to reflect reality rather than shape it. Trust slides in quietly. The abstraction "efficiency" becomes a visible behaviour: accepting defaults. "Risk" becomes a metric: a number on a screen. "Trust" becomes compliance: following the route without looking up.

The contrast with older images of divine will is instructive. Providence, in its classical formulations, did not promise optimisation. It promised meaning amid contingency. The farmer prayed for rain knowing the harvest might still fail. The pilgrim trusted guidance without expecting certainty. These frameworks preserved a gap between action and outcome, a space where responsibility and humility could coexist. Code compresses that gap. It suggests that with enough data, uncertainty can be tamed. Fate is reframed as a technical problem.

This reframing has limits, and those limits matter. A credible counter-example lies in domains where algorithmic guidance is resisted because local knowledge demonstrably outperforms it. London's black cab drivers, required to pass the Knowledge—a memorisation of over 25,000 streets—have long argued that satellite navigation degrades judgement. Studies published in *Nature Neuroscience* in 2016 by Eleanor Maguire and colleagues showed structural brain differences associated with this training. Here, human expertise resists automation not out of nostalgia but because it encodes a different kind of understanding. The reconciliation is instructive. Algorithms excel at scale and speed; humans excel at context and exception. Fate hardens when one is mistaken for the other.

Still, resistance is rare. More often, people adapt themselves to the system's expectations. Job applicants learn to tailor CVs to automated screening tools. Writers adjust headlines to please ranking algorithms. Religious leaders monitor livestream metrics to decide which messages "work". Each adjustment is rational in isolation. Together, they form a feedback loop. What is rewarded becomes what is offered. What is offered becomes what is expected. Destiny emerges not as decree but as drift.

The quiet motif threading this story is the dashboard. Dashboards promise oversight. They display the world as it supposedly is. Yet they also decide what is worth seeing. What is not measured recedes from view. Compassion, doubt, and grace do not render easily as metrics. When decisions are justified by what the dashboard shows, these unmeasured goods struggle to speak. Fate, in this sense, is not imposed by machines but negotiated through attention.

There are moments when the negotiation becomes visible. In 2018, after public concern about algorithmic bias, Amazon abandoned an internal recruitment tool that systematically downgraded CVs containing indicators of women's participation, such as attendance at women's colleges (Reuters, 2018). The system had learned from historical data that reflected past inequities. Show the behaviour: the model penalised certain terms. Name the abstraction: "meritocracy". Explain the mechanism: optimisation against biased data. Implication: when fate is learned from the past, it can reproduce injustice at speed. The counter-example does not discredit algorithms wholesale. It clarifies the moral stakes of their use.

Why, then, do people continue to speak of luck and destiny at all? Because the experience of being acted upon has not disappeared. It has changed registers. When a loan is denied, the explanation may cite a score rather than a curse, but the effect—a closed door—feels similar. When a relationship begins because two profiles were matched, the language of chance persists. People still say they were "meant to meet". Code has not erased the need for narrative. It has supplied a new grammar.

That grammar carries authority precisely because it seems impersonal. Numbers feel honest. They appear to stand above interest and interpretation. Yet this honesty is partial. Algorithms do not lie; they select. They do not judge in the human sense; they sort. When their outputs are treated as verdicts, fate hardens. When they are treated as inputs, agency survives.

The unresolved tension is this. If code is becoming a language of fate, who is fluent, and who is merely spoken about? The answer shapes whose futures feel open and whose feel foreclosed. The test ahead is not whether algorithms will guide us—they already do—but whether their guidance will be recognised as guidance rather than destiny. The next time a screen suggests a path, the question is not whether it is accurate. It is whether it is allowed to decide.

How Algorithms Actually Work

In April 2017, in Los Gatos, California, Netflix quietly changed the way it presented its recommendations. The familiar five-star rating system disappeared, replaced by a simple thumbs-up or thumbs-down. The company explained the shift in a technical blog post: users were more likely to give binary feedback, and that feedback produced cleaner data for prediction. The outcome was measurable. According to Netflix engineers, engagement increased, and recommendations became more consistent with viewing behaviour. Less choice. More signal.

Five words matter here. *Less choice. More signal.* They capture the logic that underpins most contemporary algorithms, and they do so without a single equation.

At their most basic, algorithms are not clever minds or hidden agents. They are procedures for sorting. They take inputs, apply rules, and produce outputs. What has changed in recent decades is not the existence of such procedures—merchants and bureaucrats have used them for centuries—but their scale, speed, and adaptability. Machine-learning systems do not rely on fixed instructions alone. They adjust themselves by detecting patterns across vast quantities of data. The drama lies not in intelligence, but in iteration.

To understand how this works, it helps to picture a sieve rather than a brain. Data is poured through. Some elements pass easily. Others catch. Over time, the mesh is adjusted so that what passes through aligns more closely with a chosen goal. Show the behaviour: a platform observes what people watch to completion. Name the process: pattern recognition. Explain the mechanism: correlations between past actions and future likelihoods. Implication: the system becomes better at keeping attention where it already lingers.

Prediction sits at the centre of this process. Algorithms do not know what a person will do; they estimate what a person is *likely* to do, given similarities with others and with their own past behaviour. In a streaming context, this means comparing viewing histories, time-of-day habits, device types, and abandonment points. The abstraction "preference" becomes visible behaviour: minutes watched. The abstraction "satisfaction" becomes a metric: return visits. When these proxies are fed back into the system, prediction tightens.

Optimisation then takes over. Every system is built to optimise *something*. For Netflix, it has historically been retention. For a navigation app, it may be travel time. For a credit-scoring system, default risk. Optimisation sounds neutral, but it is a moral choice disguised as arithmetic. To optimise one value is to subordinate others. A route that minimises time may increase pollution in residential streets. A feed that maximises engagement may privilege outrage over accuracy. The algorithm does not decide this. Humans do, often upstream, far from the interface where the effects are felt.

This is where judgement enters the loop. Data does not arrive labelled with meaning. Someone decides what to measure. Someone decides what to ignore. In predictive policing tools used in several US cities during the 2010s, such as those trialled in Los Angeles by the LAPD using software from PredPol, historical crime data guided patrol allocation. Studies later showed that because policing had historically focused on certain neighbourhoods, the data reflected enforcement patterns as much as crime patterns (Lum and Isaac, *Significance*, 2016). Show the behaviour: increased patrols in already-surveilled areas. Name the abstraction: "risk". Explain the mechanism: feedback from biased data. Implication: prediction can harden inequality.

A credible limitation must be acknowledged. Algorithms can outperform humans in narrow, well-defined tasks. In 2012, a team led by Geoffrey Hinton at the University of Toronto demonstrated dramatic improvements in image recognition using deep neural networks, winning the ImageNet competition. Error rates dropped sharply. In medical imaging, similar techniques have since matched or exceeded expert performance in specific diagnostic tasks, as reported by Esteva et al. in *Nature* (2017). The reconciliation is crucial. Where goals are clear, data is relevant, and feedback is reliable, algorithmic prediction can be extraordinarily effective. Problems arise when these conditions are assumed rather than tested.

The quiet motif threading this discussion is the sieve. Each pass through the system removes some possibilities and amplifies others. Over time, what remains begins to look inevitable. Yet the sieve can be reshaped. That reshaping is rarely visible to end users, which is why demystification matters. Understanding how the mesh is adjusted restores a measure of agency, even if control remains distributed.

Consider again the streaming recommendation. A viewer watches a documentary late at night and abandons it halfway through. The system records this. Was the documentary poor? Was the viewer tired? Did the interruption matter? The algorithm does not know. It treats abandonment as a signal. Multiply such assumptions across millions of users and the system converges on patterns that reflect behaviour, not intention. The abstraction "taste" is inferred from clicks. The decision to recommend or suppress certain genres follows. Over time, the catalogue itself may shift to favour content that performs well under these metrics. Choice narrows without a single decree.

This does not require malice. It requires efficiency. Efficiency is visible behaviour: fewer skipped recommendations, longer sessions, higher completion rates. Trust in the system grows because it often "gets it right". Risk appears reduced because uncertainty is smoothed. Yet something else is lost. Surprise becomes statistically inefficient. The unexpected struggles to surface because it lacks historical support. Fate, once attributed to distant forces, now emerges from aggregated habit.

Human judgement persists, but it is displaced. Engineers, product managers, and executives exercise it upstream, while users experience downstream effects as faits accomplis. Accountability becomes diffuse. When a recommendation feels constraining, there is no one to argue with. The system worked as designed. This is not destiny in the mythic sense. It is destiny as workflow.

There are countercurrents. In March 2021, Spotify announced changes to its recommendation practices to address concerns from artists about homogenisation. By adjusting how discovery playlists balanced familiarity and novelty, the company sought to expose listeners to a wider range of music. The move acknowledged a tension at the heart of optimisation. Too much prediction collapses diversity. Too little alienates users. The sieve must breathe.

The unresolved question is whether such adjustments can remain exceptional rather than structural. As algorithms continue to mediate more decisions, the temptation is to treat their outputs as answers rather than suggestions. The forward test is simple to state and difficult to practise. When a system predicts what you will choose, do you ask what it was trained to value? Or do you accept the prediction as a verdict? The difference determines whether code remains a tool—or quietly becomes fate.

Living Under Invisible Weather

On 1 June 2018, in Menlo Park, California, Facebook announced a change to its News Feed ranking intended to prioritise "meaningful social interactions". The company said users would see more posts from friends and family, fewer from publishers. Within months, traffic to many news organisations fell sharply. *Chartbeat* reported declines of over 20 per cent for some outlets. Readers noticed little. They scrolled as usual. The sky had changed. Nobody looked up.

Five short words belong here. *The weather had shifted.* Not by accident, not by decree, but by design.

Most people do not experience algorithmic systems as instructions. They experience them as conditions. Feeds refresh themselves. Timelines reorder quietly. Defaults settle into place. Like weather, these systems are ever-present and rarely questioned until something extreme occurs. A storm draws attention; a temperate climate fades into background. The danger is not that people are coerced, but that they acclimatise. Habituation dulls agency.

The social media feed offers a clear example. Show the behaviour: a user opens an app dozens of times a day, rarely scrolling beyond the first screen. Name the abstraction: attention. Explain the mechanism: ranking algorithms place content most likely to provoke reaction at the top. Implication: what is seen most often begins to feel most important. Over time, the feed becomes a proxy for reality rather than a window onto it.

Design nudges do the quiet work. Defaults matter because changing them costs effort. In 2001, economists Richard Thaler and Cass Sunstein documented how default options shape behaviour, a finding later popularised but rooted in measurable outcomes. When retirement savings plans in the United States shifted from opt-in to opt-out, participation rates rose dramatically, as reported by Madrian and Shea in the *Quarterly Journal of Economics* (2001). Show the metric:

enrolment rates increased from around 40 per cent to over 85 per cent in some firms. Name the principle: default bias. Explain the implication: when choice requires friction, passivity wins.

Digital systems exploit this insight at scale. Auto-play removes the decision to continue watching. Infinite scroll removes the stopping cue. Notification badges introduce urgency where none existed. Efficiency becomes visible behaviour: longer sessions. Trust becomes compliance: leaving settings untouched. Risk becomes a number: an alert count. None of this feels like fate. It feels natural.

The motif of invisible weather returns. Weather shapes behaviour without asking permission. People carry umbrellas because rain is expected. They do not debate the clouds. Algorithmic environments work similarly. Once a feed reliably delivers content aligned with prior engagement, curiosity narrows. The user adapts. The system learns. A loop forms.

Consider a second named example. In January 2015, Twitter introduced algorithmic timeline ranking for some users, moving away from strict chronological order. The company argued this would surface "the best Tweets". Engagement rose. By February 2016, the ranked timeline became the default for all users worldwide. Show the behaviour: fewer missed posts. Name the abstraction: relevance. Explain the mechanism: machine learning predicts which tweets matter. Implication: the present is curated before it is encountered.

What is lost is difficult to measure. Surprise resists metrics. Dissent rarely optimises engagement. Slowness has no dashboard. Yet these losses matter for agency. When the environment anticipates desire, the effort to choose otherwise increases. Passivity grows not because people stop caring, but because caring requires swimming against the current.

There is a credible counter-example. In Germany, public broadcasters such as ARD and ZDF operate under mandates that limit algorithmic personalisation in their digital offerings. By law, they must provide balanced programming accessible to all, rather than optimised for individual engagement. Usage metrics are lower than commercial platforms. Yet trust levels remain high, as reported in the Reuters Institute Digital News Report (2022). The reconciliation is instructive. Reduced optimisation trades efficiency for breadth. Weather can be moderated.

Still, most platforms prioritise scale. The economic incentives are clear. Advertising revenue tracks attention. Attention tracks habit. Habit tracks default design. The abstraction "efficiency" becomes a decision: ship the feature that reduces friction. The abstraction "choice" becomes an illusion: the option exists, but the environment discourages its use.

Invisible weather also affects moral perception. When a feed consistently amplifies certain stories, they begin to feel representative. Risk is inferred from repetition. Trust is inferred from prominence. During the COVID-19 pandemic, researchers at MIT showed that false news spread faster on Twitter than true news, driven by novelty and emotional reaction (Vosoughi, Roy, Aral, *Science*, 2018). Show the metric: speed of diffusion. Name the abstraction: credibility. Explain the mechanism: engagement signals outweigh verification. Implication: the weather favours heat over light.

Agency does not disappear under such conditions. It thins. The effort required to notice the system increases, while the reward for compliance is immediate. People still choose, but they choose within narrowed fields. Fate reappears not as command, but as constraint.

The image of weather clarifies responsibility. No single drop causes the storm. Yet storms are real. Platforms often respond to criticism by pointing to user choice. Users point to design. Both are correct, and insufficient. Responsibility diffuses across design teams, business models, and habits of use. When everyone contributes a little, accountability feels nowhere.

The unresolved tension presses forward. If algorithmic systems function as climate rather than tools, what practices help people read the weather without surrendering to it? At what point does adaptation become acquiescence? The next time a feed feels natural, the test is simple and demanding: ask what it would cost to see something else, and who decided that cost.

Meeting the Machine as Oracle

In May 2016, in Broward County, Florida, a judge considered a risk score generated by a proprietary system called COMPAS when sentencing a defendant. The score assessed the likelihood of reoffending, drawing on prior records and demographic correlations. ProPublica reported that year that the tool was more likely to falsely flag Black defendants as high risk than white defendants with similar records (Angwin et al., 2016). The score did not decide the sentence on its own. It *advised.* Yet its presence altered the room. A number spoke with confidence. The human listened.

Five words belong here. *The number spoke first.*

This is the moment where machines begin to feel like oracles. Not because they claim transcendence, but because they offer foreknowledge that appears actionable. An oracle, in ancient terms, did not coerce. It disclosed. It revealed what lay ahead, leaving humans to respond. Algorithmic systems operate in a similar register. They do not command belief. They predict behaviour, risk, preference, and propensity, then wait to be heeded. The question that presses is not whether they are accurate. It is what happens to freedom when prediction acquires authority.

Trust is the hinge. Show the behaviour: a judge consults a score; a manager follows a ranking; a parent obeys a navigation prompt. Name the abstraction: trust. Explain the mechanism: perceived objectivity, statistical grounding, institutional endorsement. Implication: the system's output becomes a reference point against which human judgement must justify itself. Silence now requires defence.

The oracle motif clarifies the shift. Classical oracles were embedded in ritual and constraint. The Delphic priestess spoke in riddles; interpretation demanded community, time, and humility. Algorithmic oracles are terse. They offer probabilities stripped of story. Their authority rests on computation rather than myth, but the effect can be similar. They shrink the field of deliberation. If the future is already legible, why argue?

A second example sharpens the point. In September 2014, in London, Google introduced predictive search suggestions that completed queries before users finished typing. The system drew on aggregated behaviour to anticipate intent. Users accepted suggestions at high rates, according to Google's own engineering reports. Show the behaviour: fewer keystrokes, faster queries. Name the abstraction: efficiency. Explain the mechanism: pattern completion. Implication: intention is shaped as it is expressed. The question you ask is nudged before it is formed.

This anticipatory logic reaches into intimate domains. Dating platforms estimate compatibility; health apps flag risk; recommendation engines infer desire. When a system seems to know us better than we know ourselves, deference feels rational. Why resist a mirror that reflects with precision? Yet the mirror is selective. It reflects what can be measured. Desire becomes a history of clicks. Risk becomes a percentile. Faith, conscience, and freedom do not disappear; they are reframed as noise around the signal.

There is a credible limitation to the oracle analogy. Algorithms do not possess intent or insight. They extrapolate. Their predictions degrade when contexts shift. During the early months of the COVID-19 pandemic in 2020, forecasting models trained on stable economic patterns failed dramatically as behaviour changed overnight. Central banks and health authorities acknowledged uncertainty publicly. Here, human judgement reasserted itself. The reconciliation matters. Oracles lose authority when their conditions break. The danger lies in forgetting those conditions exist.

The visible behaviour paired with "risk" is telling. A score reduces complexity to a threshold. Above it, caution. Below it, permission. This simplifies action but also moral reasoning. When a parole decision leans on a number, responsibility disperses. When a credit application fails an automated check, the refusal appears impersonal. Fate is experienced as procedure.

The motif returns: the oracle speaks, and the room adjusts. Screens reconfigure power. Those fluent in their language gain influence; those subject to their outputs feel judged without dialogue. This is not inevitability. It is architecture.

Faith traditions have long warned against mistaking foresight for wisdom. Foreknowledge without love was never the promise. The problem posed by algorithmic oracles is not that they know too much, but that they know *narrowly*. They see patterns, not persons. When their vision is treated as complete, freedom thins. When it is treated as partial, it can inform without ruling.

The unresolved tension presses forward into practice. Where do you already treat a system's prediction as a verdict? Notice the moment you accept a recommendation without curiosity, or decline an option because a score whispered caution. Ask, in the quiet of that acceptance, what the system was trained to value, and what it could not see. The oracle will keep speaking. The test is whether its voice becomes the last one heard.

Chapter 2
Old Stories of Fate and Freedom

In a small courtyard in ancient Jerusalem, a decision is made not by debate or vote but by lot. Stones are cast, marked pieces drawn, and the result is received not as chance but as disclosure. The Book of Proverbs would later give language to the act: *"The lot is cast into the lap, but its every decision is from the Lord."* What looks to modern eyes like randomness was, for earlier communities, a disciplined way of acknowledging limits. When human judgement reached its edge, uncertainty was not eliminated; it was ritualised. Meaning was sought not through control, but through consent to being guided.

This scene is easy to dismiss as primitive. It should not be. It reveals a sophistication that is often overlooked: a recognition that some choices are too consequential to be rushed, and too morally weighty to be reduced to preference alone. Long before algorithms, cultures wrestled with the same unease that animates our present moment. How much of a life is given, and how much is made? What does it mean to choose freely in a world that pushes back? And how does one live responsibly when outcomes are never fully known?

The temptation, when confronted with predictive systems and data-driven decisions, is to assume that the anxiety they provoke is new. It is not. What is new is the machinery. The questions are old. This chapter turns deliberately backward, not to escape the present, but to recover perspective. It explores how earlier traditions named the tension between fate, providence, and free will, and why those naming practices still matter when guidance now arrives as a score rather than a sign.

Across cultures, the patterns repeat. There are stories of destiny that cannot be avoided, and stories of tests that can be passed or failed. There are covenants that bind future action, and warnings that choices have consequences beyond intention. In Greek tragedy, the attempt to outrun fate often hastens it. In Hebrew scripture, obedience and disobedience shape history, yet always within a horizon not fully grasped. In Islamic thought, divine decree coexists with moral accountability. In Buddhist traditions, causation governs experience, yet liberation depends on disciplined response. The details differ. The structure endures.

What these traditions share is not a doctrine but a posture. Fate is never treated as an excuse. Providence does not cancel responsibility. Freedom is understood not as the absence of constraint, but as the capacity to act meaningfully within it. This is a crucial contrast with many contemporary narratives of optimisation, where constraint is framed as failure and freedom as frictionless choice. Older stories assumed friction. They built practices to meet it.

Those practices were often slow by design. Casting lots, reading omens, consulting elders, fasting, praying, waiting. Slowness was not inefficiency; it was protection. It created space for reflection, for dissent, for the unsettling possibility that desire might need examination rather than fulfilment. Decisions of vocation, marriage, or leadership were rarely made alone. Community mediated choice, not to erase individuality, but to thicken it.

The modern anxiety about determinism echoes earlier debates with striking fidelity. Philosophers have argued for centuries over whether freedom can survive causation. Augustine wrestled with grace and will; Aquinas with foreknowledge and choice; Spinoza with necessity; Kant with moral autonomy. These arguments were not academic curiosities. They shaped how people understood praise, blame, repentance, and hope. Folk wisdom carried the same tensions in simpler form: *"What will be, will be,"* set against *"You make your own luck."* Families passed down sayings that held both truths at once, without resolving them.

What has changed is the texture of being known. In earlier eras, to be known fully was to be known by God, or by a small community that shared one's history. Being known carried intimacy and risk, but also recognition. Today, being known increasingly means being modelled. Data shadows accumulate. Preferences are inferred. Likelihoods are calculated. The fear is not only that judgement has become automated, but that it has become inescapable. There is no ritual to refuse it, no sabbath from scoring.

This chapter does not attempt to adjudicate the classic arguments about free will. It uses them as a mirror. When people worry that algorithms determine their futures, they are rehearsing an old fear: that choice is an illusion, that judgement precedes action, that being known forecloses becoming. The language has changed. The unease has not.

Against this, traditions of discernment offer a counter-image. Discernment is not prediction. It does not seek certainty. It seeks faithfulness. Practices of prayer, counsel, and examination of motives assume that clarity emerges over time, through attention and honesty rather than calculation. They accept that some outcomes will remain opaque. The aim is not control, but integrity.

The contrast with modern decision aids is sharp. A recommendation promises immediacy. It reduces complexity to a ranked list. It collapses deliberation into selection. This can be helpful. It can also be corrosive. When every choice is framed as an optimisation problem, the moral dimension thins. The question shifts from *What ought I do?* to *What is most likely to work?* Older practices resisted this shift by refusing to equate success with correctness.

None of this is an argument for nostalgia. The past was not wiser by default. Omens misled. Lots were abused. Authority was oppressive as often as it was humane. The point is not to revive discarded tools, but to recover the sensibilities that animated them. Slowness. Communal accountability. An acceptance of limits. A willingness to act without guarantees.

This is why the past must be treated as a resource, not a museum. Sacred texts were never instruction manuals. They were formed through argument, revision, and lived experience. They assumed readers who would wrestle with them, not comply blindly. Terms-of-service pages, by contrast, are designed to be ignored. They demand consent without engagement. The comparison is unsettling. One invites interpretation; the other secures acquiescence. Both shape lives.

The continuity with the present moment is unmistakable. Algorithms have not invented the struggle between guidance and control. They have given it a new interface. The risk is that, dazzled by novelty, we forget the hard-won insights that earlier generations developed to live with uncertainty. The opportunity is that those insights can sharpen our response to predictive power rather than dull it.

As this chapter unfolds, readers will encounter old stories not as curiosities, but as companions. They illuminate why being guided has always been fraught, and why freedom has never meant isolation from influence. They show that the deepest human questions do not disappear when technology advances; they migrate. The task is to recognise them in their new dress.

The momentum at the end of this chapter points forward. If algorithms are the latest interpreters of uncertainty, what kind of interpreters are they? What do they amplify, and what do they ignore? And if earlier traditions insisted that guidance required discernment rather than submission, what might that insistence demand of us now? The answers will not be inherited. They will have to be practised.

Fate, Providence, and Free Will

In the early spring of around 30 CE, in Jerusalem, a small community gathered to make a decision that would shape its future. Two names were set forward to replace Judas among the Twelve. Prayer was offered. Then lots were cast. Matthias was chosen. The episode, recorded in the Acts of the Apostles, did not present the outcome as chance, nor as a vote. It presented it as disclosure. Human deliberation had reached its limit. The remainder was entrusted. The choice stood.

Five words matter here. *They consented to not knowing.*

That consent marks a pattern repeated across cultures and centuries. Long before algorithms, people faced decisions whose consequences exceeded their foresight. They sought ways to act without pretending to mastery. Fate, providence, and free will were not abstract doctrines first; they were lived tensions, negotiated through ritual, story, and habit. The tools varied—lots, omens, dreams, consultations—but the problem was shared. How does one choose when the future resists control?

In Homeric Greece, fate took the form of *moira*, a portion allotted to each life. Achilles could choose glory and early death or obscurity and long life. The choice was real. The limits were fixed. Show the scene: a hero pauses, aware of consequences. Name the abstraction: fate. Explain the structure: boundaries that constrain but do not eliminate choice. Implication: freedom operates within a given horizon, not outside it.

Hebrew scripture offers a different grammar. Covenant replaces allotment. Choices bind communities over time. Blessing and curse follow obedience and disobedience, yet outcomes are never purely mechanical. Israel wanders despite promises. Kings fall despite anointing. The abstraction "providence" becomes visible behaviour: fasting in crisis, repentance after failure, patience amid delay. The implication is moral seriousness without certainty. God's purposes are trusted, not decoded.

In Roman practice, augury and haruspicy read signs in birds or entrails before public action. These were not superstitions in the modern sense but civic technologies of decision. Show the behaviour: a magistrate postpones action after an unfavourable sign. Name the abstraction: legitimacy. Explain the mechanism: shared ritual constrains unilateral power. Implication: fate-talk can limit authority as much as justify it.

Eastern traditions frame the tension through causation rather than decree. In Buddhist thought, *karma* names the moral weight of action without positing a creator who scripts outcomes. Choices matter because they shape future conditions. Show the practice: monastic discipline ordered around intentional acts. Name the abstraction: responsibility. Explain the mechanism: causality without predestination. Implication: freedom persists, but it is educated.

These traditions disagree profoundly. Yet they converge on patterns that matter for the present. First, guidance is rarely instantaneous. Second, decisions of consequence are often communal. Third, uncertainty is not treated as a flaw to be eliminated but as a condition to be honoured. Tests and trials recur because they reveal character under pressure. Fate appears not to excuse action but to weigh it.

Philosophical debates later systematised these intuitions. Augustine wrestled with grace and will in the fifth century, insisting that divine foreknowledge did not coerce human choice. Thomas Aquinas refined the claim in the thirteenth century, distinguishing primary and secondary causes. Baruch Spinoza, writing in Amsterdam in the 1670s, denied free will in favour of necessity, yet still demanded ethical clarity. Immanuel Kant, in Königsberg in 1785, grounded freedom in moral law rather than prediction. Show the trajectory: arguments sharpen across eras. Name the abstraction: determinism. Explain the implication: responsibility survives only if action can be owned.

Folk wisdom carried the same tension without footnotes. *What's meant for you won't pass you by. You make your own luck.* Such sayings persist because they hold a contradiction people recognise. Life pushes back. Choice remains. Neither statement is sufficient alone. Together, they feel true enough to live by.

Decision tools made this tension concrete. Casting lots did not remove responsibility; it redistributed it. The community still named candidates. Prayer still framed the act. The lot entered only after discernment had done its work. Reading omens functioned similarly. It delayed action, forced attention, and made outcomes accountable to shared interpretation. Show the sequence: deliberation, ritual, acceptance. Name the abstraction: humility. Explain the mechanism: structured pause. Implication: agency is exercised without claiming sovereignty.

A credible limitation must be faced. These tools were often abused. Omens justified wars. Fate excused cruelty. Authority hid behind signs. The reconciliation lies in the pattern rather than the instrument. Where rituals narrowed power and slowed decision, they served freedom. Where they silenced dissent, they did not. The lesson transfers.

The quiet motif threading this history is the pause. A moment where action waits. In older practices, the pause was formal. Today, pauses are designed out. Instant recommendations collapse reflection into selection. The abstraction "efficiency" becomes a behaviour: clicking the first option. "Risk" becomes a threshold crossed without debate. The implication is speed without weight.

Providence, in its classical sense, did not promise outcomes aligned with preference. It promised that meaning was not exhausted by results. This matters when modern systems promise foresight. Prediction tempts us to treat likelihood as licence. Older traditions resisted that move. A test remained a test even if success was probable. A trial still demanded faithfulness.

Free will, in these stories, is neither absolute nor illusory. It is exercised under pressure. It is revealed by response. The measure of freedom is not the range of options but the integrity of choice. Visible behaviours tell the story: keeping a vow when it costs; refusing a path that promises gain at moral expense; waiting when haste would secure advantage.

The comparison with contemporary tools sharpens the stakes. When guidance arrives as a ranked list, who supplies the pause? When outcomes are framed as optimisations, who bears the weight of refusal? The past does not answer these questions. It clarifies why they matter.

Return to Jerusalem. The lot fell. Matthias was numbered among the Twelve. The community moved on, accountable to the choice it had made without pretending to control its consequences. The forward test remains with us. When faced with guidance that promises certainty, do we still know how to consent to not knowing—and to choose anyway?

Old Arguments, New Anxieties

In 1814, in Paris, Pierre-Simon Laplace published the second edition of *A Philosophical Essay on Probabilities*. In it, he described a thought experiment that would echo for centuries: an intelligence that knew the position and momentum of every particle in the universe could, in principle, predict the future entirely. Nothing would be uncertain. Past and future would lie open before it. Laplace did not claim such an intelligence existed. He used it to make a point. If causation is complete, freedom looks fragile.

Five words linger here. *Nothing would be uncertain.*

Laplace's demon was never meant to haunt kitchen tables or courtrooms. Yet the unease it crystallised has always lived there. If events follow laws, where does choice fit? If behaviour can be known in advance, what becomes of responsibility? These questions did not begin with data science, and they will not end with it. What has changed is not their substance, but their proximity. Determinism has moved from the page to the screen.

Philosophers have long staged this argument. The vocabulary shifts, the anxiety persists. Baruch Spinoza insisted that freedom was an illusion born of ignorance: people feel free because they do not know the causes that move them. David Hume countered that necessity and liberty could coexist if freedom meant acting according to one's character rather than without cause. In Königsberg in 1785, Immanuel Kant refused both positions, arguing that moral obligation presupposed freedom even if causation governed appearances. Show the debate: positions sharpen over centuries. Name the abstraction: determinism. Explain the mechanism: causal chains versus moral accountability. Implication: without freedom, praise and blame lose meaning.

These arguments were never confined to lecture halls. They seeped into ordinary speech. Families condensed them into sayings passed down with meals and admonitions. *What's meant to be won't pass you by. You reap what you sow. Do your best and leave the rest.* Such phrases do not solve the problem. They make it livable. They allow people to act without pretending to see the whole.

The family saying functions as a moral technology. It frames response. When a child fails an exam, *you did what you could* preserves dignity. When success arrives unexpectedly, *it was meant to be* restrains arrogance. Show the behaviour: consolation, restraint, perseverance.

Name the abstraction: fate. Explain the implication: destiny language absorbs shock without denying effort.

Modern data systems have revived the old anxiety under new conditions. When a credit score predicts default, when an admissions model estimates success, when a hiring algorithm ranks candidates, the question resurfaces with force. If the outcome was likely, was refusal rational? If acceptance was predicted, was effort decisive? The abstraction "risk" becomes a number. The abstraction "merit" becomes a percentile. Visible behaviour follows: applications are abandoned; appeals go unmade.

Consider a named case. In 2019, the UK government abandoned an algorithm used to allocate A-level grades after public outcry. The model, designed to prevent grade inflation during the COVID-19 pandemic, adjusted individual predictions based on a school's historical performance. High-achieving students from lower-performing schools were downgraded. Show the outcome: protests, reversals, resignations. Name the abstraction: fairness. Explain the mechanism: statistical moderation privileging history over individual performance. Implication: being known by a model felt like being judged without hearing.

The anxiety here mirrors older fears of predestination. If one's place is fixed by decree, why strive? Religious debates about election and grace wrestled with this for centuries. Some traditions emphasised assurance; others emphasised vigilance. None denied the psychological weight of being judged in advance. Data systems reintroduce that weight without offering the consolations that once accompanied it.

A second example sharpens the echo. In 2018, researchers at Stanford University published work showing that sexual orientation could be predicted from facial images with accuracy above chance using machine-learning techniques (Wang and Kosinski, *Journal of Personality and Social Psychology*). The study sparked intense criticism. Show the reaction: ethical concern, methodological dispute, public unease. Name the abstraction: privacy. Explain the mechanism: inference from patterns invisible to subjects. Implication: being known without consent revives fears of exposure once associated with divine omniscience or social surveillance.

Here lies the counter-example that demands reconciliation. Humans are not transparent even to themselves. Psychological research has long shown limits to introspection. Split-brain experiments in the 1960s, conducted by Roger Sperry and Michael Gazzaniga, demonstrated that people confabulate reasons for actions initiated without conscious awareness. If self-knowledge is partial, predictive systems may sometimes see regularities we overlook. The reconciliation is not to grant them authority, but to recognise the asymmetry. Knowing patterns is not knowing persons.

The motif threading these arguments is judgement. Who judges, by what standard, and with what consequences? In older frameworks, judgement was often deferred or distributed. Divine judgement lay beyond human reach. Communal judgement was tempered by relationship. Data-driven judgement is immediate and scalable. It acts now. The room changes when it speaks.

Trust follows judgement closely. Trust in a system grows when it performs reliably. Efficiency reinforces that trust. A navigation app that saves ten minutes earns obedience. The visible metric—arrival time—stands in for wisdom. Over time, the habit of deference forms. When the system errs, the surprise feels personal. The user trusted. The abstraction "efficiency" becomes a behaviour: following the route without question.

Folk wisdom anticipates this danger. *Measure twice, cut once. Don't put all your eggs in one basket.* These sayings warn against single sources of authority. They preserve plurality. The endurance of such phrases suggests that people have always known the risk of over-confidence in any one guide, whether divine, rational, or technical.

What data systems add is velocity. Old arguments unfolded over lifetimes. New anxieties arrive before breakfast. Being known and judged now happens continuously, often invisibly. The temptation is to resolve the discomfort by declaring the debate obsolete. *The data speaks.* It does not. It computes.

Return to Laplace. His demon was a thought experiment, not a programme. He knew the limits of the claim. Modern systems are more modest, yet more intrusive. They do not promise total knowledge. They promise enough. Enough to influence action. Enough to feel decisive. Enough to unsettle freedom.

The unresolved tension remains. If prediction grows more accurate, does responsibility shrink? Or does responsibility shift to how predictions are used, resisted, or ignored? The forward test is lived rather than answered. The next time a number seems to know you, notice whether it invites reflection or demands compliance. Old arguments are not settled. They are rehearsed, again, in a new key.

Discernment Before Data

In March 1522, in the small Catalan town of Manresa, Ignatius of Loyola laid down his sword. Wounded months earlier at Pamplona, he had retreated first into recovery and then into reflection. At Manresa, he began to record the inner movements of fear, desire, consolation, and resistance that accompanied his decisions. Those notes would later become the *Spiritual Exercises*, a practical guide to discernment that has shaped centuries of vocational choice within the Jesuit tradition and beyond. Ignatius did not ask for certainty. He trained attention.

Five words matter here. *He learned to wait.*

The scene is distant, yet recognisable. A person faces a life-defining choice without reliable forecasts. The response is not calculation, but practice. Discernment, as Ignatius understood it, was not mystical guesswork. It was a disciplined way of noticing what kinds of choices led toward coherence and what kinds led toward fragmentation. The future remained opaque. The task was to choose faithfully within that opacity.

Religious traditions across cultures developed similar practices, though with different vocabularies. Prayer, counsel, fasting, silence, confession, and communal deliberation all served a common purpose: to slow the moment of decision so that desire could be examined rather than obeyed. Show the behaviour: delaying commitment. Name the abstraction: discernment. Explain the mechanism: structured attention to motives and consequences over time. Implication: freedom deepens when choice is tested rather than rushed.

High-stakes decisions were rarely treated as private acts. Choosing a vocation, a partner, or a place to belong was embedded in community. Elders questioned motives. Friends observed patterns. Rituals marked thresholds. The abstraction "trust" became visible behaviour: submitting one's intention to scrutiny. The abstraction "risk" became a shared burden: consequences were borne together.

Contrast this with modern decision aids. A recommendation engine presents ranked options instantly. A compatibility score reduces relational complexity to a percentage. Efficiency becomes the governing value. The visible metric is speed: decisions made in minutes rather than months. The implication is not that such tools are useless, but that they bypass a form of wisdom that older practices insisted upon. Slowness was not inefficiency. It was discernment's condition.

Consider a concrete contrast. In many Christian communities until the nineteenth century, choosing a vocation involved extended periods of testing. Novitiates lasted years. Candidates lived under rule before commitment. Behaviour was observed. Patterns emerged. The cost was time. The benefit was depth. Today, vocational guidance often arrives through aptitude tests and labour-market analytics. Show the behaviour: selecting a career path based on predicted fit. Name the abstraction: optimisation. Explain the mechanism: matching traits to outcomes. Implication: suitability replaces calling.

The same contrast appears in partner selection. Anthropological studies of arranged marriages, such as those documented by anthropologist Serena Nanda in India in the late twentieth century, show that compatibility was assessed through family networks, reputation, and shared obligations. Divorce rates were lower, though at the cost of individual autonomy. In contrast, dating apps rank potential partners using behavioural data and stated preferences.

Show the behaviour: swiping. Name the abstraction: choice. Explain the mechanism: abundance framed as freedom. Implication: commitment becomes provisional.

A credible limitation must be faced. Discernment practices could entrench conformity and suppress dissent. Communities misread motives. Elders abused authority. The reconciliation lies in distinguishing discernment from control. At its best, discernment invites examination rather than enforcement. It asks whether a choice leads toward integrity over time, not whether it conforms immediately.

The quiet motif threading this comparison is time. Discernment stretches it. Data compresses it. When time is compressed, decisions feel decisive before they are understood. When time is stretched, uncertainty becomes bearable. The abstraction "patience" becomes a behaviour: waiting through ambiguity. The abstraction "confidence" becomes a decision: committing without guarantees.

Modern systems often treat uncertainty as a problem to eliminate. Predictive tools promise foresight. Risk calculators promise reassurance. Yet many religious traditions treated uncertainty as spiritually formative. Not knowing forced reliance, humility, and attentiveness. The future's opacity was not an enemy; it was a teacher. Show the practice: fasting before a decision. Name the abstraction: humility. Explain the mechanism: embodied dependence. Implication: agency is exercised without mastery.

This difference matters when recommendation systems shape choice environments. A system trained to maximise engagement will privilege options similar to past selections. Novelty appears risky. Discernment practices, by contrast, often valued disruption. A call was recognised precisely because it unsettled. The visible behaviour was resistance to ease. The implication was transformation.

There are modern attempts to recover this sensibility. In 2019, some professional schools reintroduced extended reflective components into admissions and training, responding to evidence that purely metric-driven selection correlated weakly with long-term satisfaction. Studies in organisational psychology, such as those by

Amy Wrzesniewski on "job crafting", show that meaning emerges through reflection and adaptation rather than initial fit. The reconciliation is partial but instructive. Data can inform. It cannot replace discernment.

Ignatius' notes from Manresa did not predict his future influence. They trained his attention. The Exercises ask participants to notice recurring patterns over weeks: what leads to peace, what to restlessness. The visible behaviour is journalling. The abstraction "calling" becomes a trajectory rather than a moment. Implication: choice unfolds.

The unresolved tension presses forward. Instant recommendations are seductive because they relieve the burden of waiting. Discernment demands endurance. When faced with a choice that matters, the question is not whether data is available. It is whether time is allowed. The next decision will test this. Will speed be treated as wisdom, or will waiting be permitted to teach?

The Past as Resource, Not Museum

On 9 January 2007, in San Francisco, Steve Jobs stood on a stage and introduced the iPhone. He described it as a device that would collapse tools into one interface and make interaction "natural". The applause was immediate. What followed was less visible. Over the next decade, terms-of-service agreements lengthened, scrolled past by millions with a thumb flick. Consent was given without reading. The device promised intuition. The contract demanded surrender.

Five words linger here. *Nobody read the text.*

This is not a story about carelessness. It is a story about how guidance is framed. Sacred texts were rarely meant to be consumed quickly. They assumed rereading, argument, commentary, and communal interpretation. Their authority grew through engagement. Terms-of-service pages assume the opposite. They are designed to be bypassed. Their authority depends on acquiescence. The contrast is not about old versus new. It is about how the past treated uncertainty as something to be wrestled with, while many contemporary systems treat it as something to be managed away.

Algorithms did not invent the struggle between guidance and control. They inherited it. Every culture has faced moments when the desire for certainty collided with the reality of limited knowledge. The difference lies in how those cultures responded. Some built practices that slowed decision-making and distributed responsibility. Others centralised authority and accelerated action. The past is not a museum of obsolete answers. It is a catalogue of strategies tested under pressure.

Consider the medieval practice of glossing scripture. In twelfth-century Paris, scholars such as Peter Lombard compiled commentaries that layered interpretation upon interpretation. A text was not finished when written. It lived through use. Show the behaviour: marginal notes accumulate. Name the abstraction: authority. Explain the mechanism: authority emerges through sustained engagement. Implication: guidance invites participation rather than compliance.

Now contrast this with a modern platform update. In August 2018, Facebook revised its data policy in response to the Cambridge Analytica scandal. The document ran to thousands of words. Users were required to click "Agree" to continue. Show the behaviour: rapid acceptance. Name the abstraction: consent. Explain the mechanism: access conditioned on agreement. Implication: control consolidates when engagement is impractical.

The motif threading this section is the text. Who reads it? Who writes it? Who can argue with it? Sacred texts assumed disputation. The Talmud preserves minority opinions alongside majority rulings. Islamic jurisprudence records disagreement as a sign of vitality. Protestant traditions fractured precisely because texts were placed in lay hands. These practices did not eliminate authority. They complicated it.

A second named example clarifies the point. In 1215, at Runnymede in England, King John sealed Magna Carta. The document limited royal power and affirmed that even the sovereign stood under law.

Show the outcome: barons compel assent. Name the abstraction: accountability. Explain the mechanism: written constraint open to appeal. Implication: guidance can bind the powerful as well as the weak.

This history matters when algorithms function as interpreters of uncertainty. Predictive systems translate ambiguity into scores. They offer guidance that feels definitive because it is quantified. The past offers a caution. Quantification has always tempted rulers. Medieval astrological charts guided political decisions. Renaissance princes consulted them before war. The practice faded not because uncertainty disappeared, but because its limits were exposed. Predictions failed. Authority shifted.

A credible counter-example must be faced. The past also produced fatalism. Caste systems hardened destiny into birthright. Doctrines of predestination were used to justify hierarchy. The reconciliation lies in how traditions corrected themselves. Reform movements arose. New readings challenged old ones. The past is a resource precisely because it includes its own critiques.

The abstraction "trust" becomes visible behaviour in these moments. People trusted texts they could argue with more than edicts they could not. Efficiency was not the goal. Legitimacy was. Modern systems invert the priority. Efficiency becomes visible behaviour: faster decisions, fewer appeals. Legitimacy is assumed to follow. The risk is quiet erosion.

Return to the contrast between sacred texts and terms-of-service pages. One demands time. The other demands speed. One expects interpretation. The other forbids it. One grows through commentary. The other hides behind legal necessity. The provocative question is not which is more truthful. It is which forms people capable of judgement.

Algorithms, like texts, encode values. They are written by people, trained on histories, deployed within institutions. Treating them as neutral tools repeats an old mistake: mistaking form for authority. The past offers a different stance. Treat guidance as provisional. Subject it to communal testing. Allow dissent to surface.

There are modern attempts to do this. In 2020, the European Union proposed the Artificial Intelligence Act, introducing requirements for transparency and contestability in high-risk systems. Show the behaviour: documentation mandates. Name the abstraction: oversight. Explain the mechanism: making systems legible to regulators. Implication: authority is checked by process. The effort is incomplete, but it echoes older instincts.

The past also reminds us that guidance is relational. Covenants bound people together over time. Laws assumed memory. Algorithms operate in an eternal present, updating continuously. The abstraction "responsibility" becomes visible behaviour when consequences unfold slowly and are remembered. When systems forget yesterday's context, accountability thins.

The unresolved tension remains. If algorithms are the latest interpreters of uncertainty, will they be treated as texts to be argued with or as contracts to be accepted? The next click will answer, briefly, before the screen refreshes.

Chapter 3
Inside the Black Box

On a Tuesday morning, a letter arrives that does not look like a judgement. It is polite, brief, and definitive. *We regret to inform you…* No explanation follows, only a reference number and a suggestion to reapply in six months. Somewhere in the background, a decision has been made. No person appears to have made it. There is no desk to visit, no official to persuade, no story to tell. The door is simply closed.

For many people, this is now the texture of power. Decisions that shape livelihoods, mobility, and dignity arrive without faces. They are delivered as outcomes, not arguments. When asked how the decision was reached, the answer, if it comes at all, gestures toward a system: a model, a score, a process too complex to summarise. The box is black not because it is malicious, but because it is opaque by design.

Opacity has always unsettled human beings. Ancient societies surrounded power with ritual to make it legible, even when it was feared. Modern bureaucracies surrounded power with paperwork to make it accountable, even when it was slow. Algorithmic systems promise something different: speed without explanation, accuracy without narrative. This chapter enters that promise with care, not to expose secrets, but to ask what is gained and what is lost when judgement is hidden inside machinery.

The phrase *black box* is borrowed from engineering. It describes a system whose internal workings are not visible, even if its inputs and outputs are known. In aviation, black boxes exist to preserve truth after disaster. In algorithmic life, they exist as a condition of everyday operation. We interact with them constantly, trusting that what goes in is treated fairly and that what comes out is justified. Trust, here, is not relational. It is procedural.

This chapter opens that box in plain language. Not to impress, but to orient. It begins with how raw data becomes a score: how fragments of past behaviour are collected, labelled, and assembled into predictions about future action. The emphasis is not on technical brilliance, but on trade-offs. Every choice about data involves inclusion and exclusion. Every model privileges certain patterns over others. An example from credit scoring makes this concrete, tracing how financial histories become proxies for trustworthiness, and how yesterday's circumstances can quietly govern tomorrow's options.

From there, attention turns to feedback loops, the quiet engines that make prediction self-confirming. When a system treats someone as risky, opportunities narrow. When opportunities narrow, behaviour adapts. The next round of data then appears to justify the original judgement. This is not conspiracy. It is momentum. The chapter follows a single story—a job applicant repeatedly filtered out before reaching human review—to show how self-fulfilling code forms, and why it is so difficult to interrupt once it is in motion. The logic echoes ancient warnings about beliefs that shape the realities they claim merely to observe.

Opacity deepens when systems become complex enough that even their creators struggle to explain specific outcomes. This is not incompetence; it is a feature of certain machine-learning approaches that trade interpretability for performance. The result is a new kind of mystery. Not the mystery of divine will, which traditions surrounded with humility and prayer, but the mystery of statistical correlation, surrounded by confidence and scale. The chapter compares these two kinds of mystery carefully, resisting easy analogies. One invites trust through relationship. The other demands trust through abstraction.

To make the distinction tangible, the chapter introduces a simple image: sealed boxes and open ledgers. Sealed boxes deliver results without accounts. Open ledgers expose process, even when the process is imperfect. Modern societies are increasingly governed by sealed boxes, not because transparency is impossible, but because it is inconvenient. The question is not whether all systems can be fully explained. It is whether explanation is treated as a moral requirement or an optional courtesy.

This leads to the hardest question of the chapter: accountability without a single author. Algorithmic decisions are rarely the work of one mind. They emerge from teams, datasets, incentives, and infrastructures spread across institutions. When harm occurs, responsibility fragments. Engineers point to policy. Organisations point to vendors. Vendors point to models. Models point to data. The circle closes without an answer. A case of wrongful denial of essential services grounds this discussion, showing how abstraction translates into human cost when no one can be clearly addressed.

Yet this chapter is not an indictment. It is an invitation to look more closely at how power now operates. The black box is not a monster. It is a mirror of our priorities. Speed over explanation. Scale over judgement. Efficiency over repair. These are choices, even when they are embedded deeply enough to feel inevitable.

The chapter's purpose is to equip readers with a way of seeing. To recognise where trade-offs are being made. To notice when mystery is being used to foreclose accountability rather than to cultivate humility. To ask, with seriousness rather than suspicion, who bears responsibility when decisions are distributed across systems that no one fully controls.

The pages that follow will not teach readers how to build models. They will teach readers how to read them. They will move slowly through processes often presented as magical or forbidding, insisting that clarity is possible without reduction. They will show why understanding feedback loops matters for justice, why opacity challenges trust differently than older forms of mystery, and why accountability must be reimagined when authorship dissolves.

The tension at the end of this chapter remains unresolved, and deliberately so. If the most consequential judgements of our time are made inside boxes we cannot easily open, what kind of trust is being asked of us? And what kind of responsibility are we willing to demand in return?

From Raw Data to Scores

In 1989, in Minneapolis, the Fair Isaac Corporation introduced what it called the FICO score. Banks had long judged borrowers through interviews and paper trails, but this was different. A single number, derived from past repayment behaviour, would summarise risk. Lenders adopted it quickly. By the mid-1990s it shaped millions of decisions each year. Credit became faster to grant and easier to refuse. Lives adjusted accordingly.

Five words belong here. *The past predicts the future.*

That promise sits at the heart of most scoring systems. They do not claim certainty. They claim likelihood. What they require, before any calculation begins, is data—pieces of the past rendered legible enough to be counted. Opening the black box starts there, not with mathematics, but with selection. What is noticed. What is ignored. What is deemed relevant enough to record.

Data does not fall from the sky. It is collected through transactions, sensors, forms, and traces of behaviour left behind as people move through systems. In credit scoring, the visible behaviours are concrete: bills paid on time, balances carried, credit limits used, accounts opened. Each behaviour becomes a variable. Trust, an abstraction, becomes a payment history. Risk becomes utilisation ratios. Responsibility becomes a record of defaults. The implication is immediate. Character is inferred from conduct that can be measured.

Before models ever run, data is labelled. Someone decides what counts as success and failure. In lending, repayment on schedule becomes "good". Missed payments become "bad". These labels feel obvious until edge cases appear. A missed payment due to illness looks identical to one due to negligence. The system does not know the difference. It is not built to. The trade-off is efficiency for nuance.

Once labelled, data is fed into models that compare patterns across populations. A borrower's history is set alongside millions of others.

Similarities are counted. Differences weighted. The model estimates how often people with comparable patterns defaulted in the past. That frequency becomes a score. Show the process: past behaviour grouped and averaged. Name the abstraction: prediction. Explain the mechanism: statistical correlation. Implication: individuality thins into category.

The credit score's power lies in its portability. A three-digit number travels easily across institutions. It standardises judgement. Lenders trust it because it simplifies decision-making and reduces perceived risk. The visible metric—default rates—justifies its use. According to the Consumer Financial Protection Bureau, lenders using credit scores reduced manual underwriting costs significantly in the 1990s. Efficiency rewarded adoption.

A second named example illustrates the spread. In the United Kingdom, Experian expanded consumer credit scoring through the 2000s, integrating electoral roll data and utility records. The place matters. Public data becomes private judgement. Show the behaviour: registering to vote improves creditworthiness. Name the abstraction: civic participation. Explain the mechanism: data linkage. Implication: social actions acquire financial consequences.

The quiet motif threading this process is the ledger. Each action is written down. Ledgers promise memory. They also freeze context. Once entered, an item persists beyond the circumstances that produced it. A late payment remains late long after the crisis that caused it passes. The ledger does not forget. It recalculates.

There are benefits that should not be minimised. Scoring systems reduced arbitrary discrimination by replacing subjective impressions with consistent criteria. Studies by the Federal Reserve in the early 2000s showed expanded access to credit for some previously excluded borrowers. The counter-example matters. Human judgement is not neutral either. Bias did not begin with data.

Yet limitations are structural. Models inherit the past they are trained on. If historical access to credit was uneven, predictions reflect that unevenness. In 2013, researchers at the Federal Reserve Bank of Boston showed that credit scores correlated strongly with income and neighbourhood, variables shaped by decades of policy. Show the outcome: higher interest rates for certain postcodes. Name the abstraction: fairness. Explain the mechanism: proxy variables stand in for protected characteristics. Implication: inequality reproduces itself quietly.

Trade-offs appear everywhere. Including more data may improve accuracy but deepen intrusion. Excluding certain variables may protect privacy but reduce performance. Designers choose. Institutions choose. These choices are rarely visible to those scored. The abstraction "trust" becomes a decision by lenders to accept the number. The abstraction "agency" becomes a borrower's limited ability to contest it.

The black box feels forbidding because the path from behaviour to score is indirect. A person knows they paid a bill late. They do not see how that event interacts with dozens of others to move a score by twenty points. The system measures, compares, commits. Explanation arrives, if at all, as a list of factors, not a narrative.

A credible limitation complicates the critique. Some behaviours predict outcomes reliably. Payment history is a strong indicator of future repayment. Removing it would increase defaults, raising costs for all borrowers. The reconciliation lies in recognising that accuracy does not exhaust justice. A model can be correct and still harmful if its outputs are treated as destiny rather than input.

The ledger metaphor returns when scores are used beyond lending. Employers screen candidates. Landlords vet tenants. Insurers price premiums. A score built for one purpose migrates to others. Show the behaviour: automated screening before interviews. Name the abstraction: suitability. Explain the mechanism: risk aversion scaled. Implication: opportunities narrow upstream.

Opacity compounds the effect. Proprietary models are protected as trade secrets. Individuals cannot see the full ledger, only its summary. Appeals are limited. The abstraction "accountability" becomes a procedural maze. Responsibility diffuses.

Yet the box is not sealed by necessity. Some jurisdictions have demanded explanation. The European Union's General Data Protection Regulation, enacted in 2018, granted individuals rights to information about automated decisions. Show the behaviour: disclosure notices. Name the abstraction: transparency. Explain the mechanism: legal constraint. Implication: explanation becomes a requirement, not a courtesy. The effort remains uneven, but the principle stands.

What emerges from this walk-through is not a tale of villainy or genius. It is a story of translation. Human lives are translated into data. Data into labels. Labels into scores. Scores into decisions. At each step, something is gained and something is lost. Speed is gained. Context is lost. Consistency is gained. Particularity is lost.

The unresolved tension presses forward. If scores condense the past into guidance for the future, how much weight should they carry? The next time a number stands in for a person, the question is not whether the number is wrong. It is whether it is allowed to be final.

Feedback Loops and Self-Fulfilling Code

In February 2018, in New York City, Amazon quietly scrapped an internal hiring system it had been developing for several years. The tool, trained on past CVs submitted to the company, learned to downgrade applications that resembled those historically hired—most of whom were men. Resumes containing terms associated with women's colleges or female-coded experience were scored lower. The system did not intend discrimination. It mirrored success. The outcome was predictable. The future was trained to look like the past.

Five words matter here. *The system learned history.*

Feedback loops begin with a promise: prediction improves with experience. The more a system sees, the better it should become. This is often true in bounded environments. Yet when predictions influence the very behaviour they claim to observe, learning becomes circular. The model shapes the world it measures. Over time, description hardens into prescription.

A feedback loop forms when three elements align. First, a system predicts an outcome. Second, that prediction influences decisions. Third, those decisions generate new data that confirms the original prediction. Show the behaviour: candidates are filtered out before interview. Name the abstraction: risk management. Explain the mechanism: past hiring patterns define "fit". Implication: opportunity narrows along familiar lines.

The logic is quiet. No single decision appears unjust. Each step seems rational. A recruiter relies on a ranking to manage volume. The ranking reflects past success. The system updates itself based on who was hired and who was not. Over time, those excluded accumulate fewer chances to demonstrate competence. The absence of evidence becomes evidence of absence.

This dynamic is not confined to hiring. In lending, borrowers with higher credit scores receive better terms. Better terms reduce default risk. Reduced risk feeds back into higher scores. Those with lower scores face higher costs, increasing strain and default likelihood. Show the metric: interest rates rise with risk bands. Name the abstraction: fairness. Explain the mechanism: preferential treatment compounds advantage. Implication: inequality stabilises itself.

The phrase *self-fulfilling prophecy* predates code. Sociologist Robert K. Merton coined it in 1948 to describe beliefs that bring about their own confirmation. If a bank run is feared, depositors withdraw funds. The bank collapses. The belief was false, then true. Algorithms operationalise this phenomenon at scale. They do not merely observe behaviour. They participate in its formation.

A single story brings the loop into focus. Consider a job applicant applying to large firms through automated screening tools. Each rejection is invisible. No feedback arrives. The applicant's CV remains unchanged. The system records non-selection. Over time, the applicant's profile diverges further from those marked as successful. When a human finally reviews the application, gaps appear. The system predicted low fit. It helped produce it.

Spiritual traditions have long warned against such loops. Beliefs, they argued, shape conduct, which shapes character. In the Christian tradition, despair is named a vice not because suffering is illusory, but because hopelessness constrains action. In Buddhism, attachment to fixed identity reinforces suffering. The insight is shared: what one expects to be true often governs what becomes possible.

The analogy is not perfect. Algorithms lack intention. They do not hope or despair. Yet the pattern holds. Treat someone as untrustworthy, and you reduce the chances they will prove otherwise. Treat a neighbourhood as risky, and you increase surveillance, which increases recorded incidents, which justifies further surveillance. In 2016, researchers Kristian Lum and William Isaac demonstrated this effect in predictive policing models (*Significance*), showing how feedback loops reinforced racial bias even with neutral inputs. Show the outcome: arrest data concentrates. Name the abstraction: public safety. Explain the mechanism: enforcement shapes data. Implication: prediction replaces judgement.

Efficiency drives these loops. Systems are praised for reducing uncertainty. Managers trust them because they appear consistent. Trust becomes visible behaviour: deference to scores. The more decisions rely on the system, the more influence it exerts. Over time, human discretion atrophies. The loop tightens.

A credible counter-example matters. Not all feedback loops are harmful. In recommender systems for music discovery, positive feedback can broaden exposure when designed deliberately. Spotify's adjustments to its Discover Weekly playlist in 2019 aimed to balance familiarity with exploration, countering homogenisation. Show the behaviour: inclusion of unfamiliar artists. Name the abstraction: diversity. Explain the mechanism: weighting novelty. Implication: loops can be redirected.

The reconciliation lies in design and governance. Feedback loops are not inevitable; they are engineered. Choices about what counts as success, how often models retrain, and whether negative outcomes are interrogated shape the loop's direction. When systems are optimised solely for short-term metrics, loops accelerate. When they are constrained by external values, loops can loosen.

The quiet motif threading this section is the echo. A sound reflects off a surface and returns altered but recognisable. The first signal matters disproportionately. In social systems, early advantage echoes loudly. Late correction struggles to register.

Opacity amplifies the effect. Individuals subject to feedback loops rarely see them. They experience outcomes, not processes. Appeals are limited because causation is diffuse. The abstraction "accountability" becomes a maze of references. Each component worked as intended. The system as a whole did not.

There are historical precedents. In the early twentieth century, intelligence testing was used to sort students and soldiers. Early results shaped expectations, which shaped training, which shaped outcomes. Critics such as Walter Lippmann warned that measurement would be mistaken for destiny. The tests fell out of favour not because measurement failed, but because the loops were exposed.

The spiritual warning embedded here is not against knowledge, but against premature closure. When belief calcifies, repentance becomes impossible. When prediction forecloses possibility, freedom thins. Traditions that prized conversion and forgiveness did so because they resisted final judgements. A person was more than their past.

Algorithmic systems struggle with this principle. They are built to remember. Forgetting is costly. Yet moral life depends on the possibility of change. Visible behaviour—second chances—becomes rare when systems lack memory for transformation. Metrics lag reality.

Some jurisdictions have begun to respond. "Right to explanation" provisions and calls for algorithmic impact assessments aim to surface loops before they entrench. Show the behaviour: audits conducted. Name the abstraction: oversight. Explain the mechanism: external review interrupts automation. Implication: feedback can be questioned.

The unresolved tension remains practical. Prediction improves decisions until it begins to govern them. The forward test is not theoretical. When a system's output confirms itself, do we accept the echo as truth—or do we listen for what it has learned to ignore?

Opacity, Mystery, and Trust

In October 2015, in Austin, Texas, a software engineer named Alex was struck and killed by a self-driving test vehicle operated by Uber. The company paused its programme, issued statements, and released partial technical explanations. Investigators later concluded that the system had detected the pedestrian but failed to classify her in time to respond. No single line of code could be blamed. Responsibility dissolved into architecture.

Five words matter here. *Nobody fully understood it.*

Opacity unsettles because it disrupts the moral grammar people rely on to assign trust and blame. When harm occurs and no clear author can be named, the familiar routes to accountability close. The decision was made, but not by a person in the usual sense. It emerged from a system whose internal reasoning resisted narration. The black box did not merely hide information. It changed how responsibility could be imagined.

Many contemporary algorithmic systems are opaque for reasons that have little to do with secrecy. Some are opaque because they are proprietary, protected as commercial assets. Others are opaque because they are complex beyond intuitive grasp. Deep neural networks, for example, adjust millions of parameters during training. Engineers can observe performance improvements without being able to trace a specific output back to a human-readable rule. Show the behaviour: a model flags a case as high risk. Name the abstraction: explainability. Explain the mechanism: non-linear interactions resist summary. Implication: justification thins into assurance.

Opacity shifts trust from understanding to outcome. When systems perform well, trust grows. When they fail, trust collapses abruptly. The visible metric—accuracy rates—stands in for comprehension. According to a 2019 study by Doshi-Velez and Kim in *Communications of the ACM*, practitioners often accept opaque models because they outperform interpretable ones on benchmark tasks. Efficiency wins. Understanding waits.

This posture has precedents. Human societies have always lived with mystery. Divine providence, natural forces, and human psychology have resisted full explanation. Faith traditions developed languages to live with this resistance without surrendering moral seriousness. Mystery was not ignorance to be erased, but depth to be respected. Crucially, mystery was accompanied by practices of trust anchored in relationship.

The comparison with inscrutable code is tempting and dangerous. Both present outcomes without full explanation. Both ask for trust. Yet the limits matter. Providence, in its classical sense, was not accountable to performance metrics. It was accountable to character. Trust was relational, tested over time through fidelity rather than optimisation. Algorithmic systems ask for trust based on output quality and institutional endorsement. The difference is not theological. It is ethical.

The image of sealed boxes versus open ledgers helps clarify this distinction. A sealed box delivers a result. An open ledger records how that result was reached. Modern algorithmic systems often function as sealed boxes. Inputs go in. Outputs come out. Explanations, if offered, are post hoc summaries. The ledger remains closed.

This closure has consequences. In 2016, ProPublica investigated the COMPAS risk assessment tool used in US courts. Defendants could not see how scores were calculated. Judges could not interrogate the model's reasoning. Show the outcome: sentencing decisions influenced by opaque scores. Name the abstraction: legitimacy. Explain the mechanism: authority asserted without transparency. Implication: trust is demanded rather than earned.

A second named example sharpens the point. In 2020, the UK's Department for Work and Pensions used automated systems to detect benefit fraud. Claimants reported account suspensions without clear explanations. Appeals were slow. The system's criteria were not disclosed. Show the behaviour: payments halted. Name the abstraction: risk management. Explain the mechanism: automated flagging prioritises false positives over false negatives. Implication: vulnerability increases where explanation is absent.

The abstraction "trust" becomes a behaviour here. People comply because resistance is costly. They accept outcomes because appeal paths are obscure. Trust mutates into resignation. The fear is not that power is exercised, but that it is faceless. When no one can explain a decision, no one can be persuaded.

A credible limitation must be acknowledged. Full transparency is not always possible or desirable. Revealing every detail of a fraud-detection system can enable gaming. Explaining every parameter of a complex model may mislead rather than clarify. The reconciliation lies in distinguishing transparency from intelligibility. An open ledger does not require raw data dumps. It requires reasons that can be questioned.

Some fields have begun to explore this distinction. In medicine, explainable AI research aims to provide clinicians with interpretable signals rather than raw scores. A 2018 study by Ribeiro, Singh, and Guestrin proposed methods for explaining model predictions locally (*KDD Proceedings*). Show the behaviour: highlighting influential features. Name the abstraction: accountability. Explain the mechanism: partial explanation supports judgement. Implication: trust becomes collaborative.

The spiritual analogy returns here with caution. Mystery, in religious traditions, was often paired with lament. People protested divine silence. They argued. They refused easy answers. Sacred texts preserve these arguments. The Book of Job is an extended dispute with unexplained suffering. Mystery did not foreclose dialogue. It provoked it.

Algorithmic opacity often does the opposite. It forecloses dialogue by rendering questions illegible. A system cannot be cross-examined. Its designers are distant. The institution defers to the model. The abstraction "responsibility" becomes a relay. Each actor passes it along.

The ledger metaphor clarifies what is at stake. Open ledgers allow errors to be traced. Sealed boxes demand faith in process. Faith, here, is not a virtue. It is a necessity imposed by design. The risk is that habituation normalises this necessity.

There are efforts to reopen the ledger. The European Union's proposed AI regulations emphasise risk classification and documentation. Audits, model cards, and impact assessments aim to surface assumptions. Show the behaviour: compliance reports generated. Name the abstraction: governance. Explain the mechanism: procedural transparency. Implication: trust is scaffolded rather than assumed.

Yet governance alone cannot answer the deeper unease. Even a well-documented system may remain difficult to explain. The question then shifts. When explanation fails, what anchors trust? In older frameworks, trust rested on shared narratives and moral commitments. In modern systems, it rests on performance and legality. Both are fragile.

Return to Austin. The investigation concluded. Testing resumed. The sealed box was adjusted. For those affected, explanation arrived too late. The unresolved tension persists. When power speaks through systems we cannot fully understand, what kind of trust is reasonable—and what kind of accountability must be insisted upon before we accept the answer and move on?

Accountability Without a Single Author

In October 2013, in Michigan, the state's Unemployment Insurance Agency deployed an automated fraud-detection system known as MiDAS. Within months, thousands of claimants received letters accusing them of fraud, demanding repayment with penalties of up to 400 per cent. Many were wrong. By 2015, investigative reporting by *The Detroit Free Press* revealed that the system had falsely accused more than 20,000 people. Homes were seized. Wages were garnished. Lives were upended. When the errors came to light, an unsettling fact followed. No single official could explain how each decision had been made.

Five words belong here. *Everyone touched it; nobody owned it.*

This is the moral terrain of algorithmic governance. Decisions emerge from systems assembled by many hands and guided by dispersed intentions. Data scientists design models. Agencies set thresholds. Contractors integrate software. Caseworkers rely on outputs. Each step appears reasonable. Harm accumulates anyway. Accountability, once anchored to identifiable authors, begins to dissolve into process.

The Michigan case makes the human cost of abstraction visible. Show the behaviour: automated flags trigger repayment demands without review. Name the abstraction: fraud prevention. Explain the mechanism: rules and models prioritise false positives to save money. Implication: error shifts from exception to burden borne by the vulnerable. When claimants appealed, they encountered call centres and forms, not decision-makers. The system answered for itself.

Accountability has always been a social achievement rather than a given. In law, responsibility is assigned to persons because persons can answer questions, explain reasons, and accept consequences. Systems complicate this arrangement. When outcomes are produced by interactions among code, data, and policy, responsibility fragments. Each actor can point elsewhere. The result is a gap where moral repair should be.

A second named example sharpens the picture. In 2020, in the Netherlands, the government resigned after revelations about the childcare benefits scandal. An algorithmic risk model used by the tax authority disproportionately flagged families with dual nationality for fraud. Thousands were wrongly accused. Debts mounted. Trust collapsed. Show the outcome: cabinet resignation. Name the abstraction: risk scoring. Explain the mechanism: proxy variables entangled with nationality. Implication: discrimination emerged without explicit intent.

These cases expose a paradox. The more distributed a decision becomes, the harder it is to locate accountability. Yet distribution is precisely what makes modern systems efficient. Efficiency becomes visible behaviour: faster processing, fewer staff. The abstraction "responsibility" becomes a checklist item rather than a lived obligation.

Legal systems are beginning to grapple with this shift. Traditional liability assumes a chain of causation that can be traced. Algorithmic decisions complicate causation. Was harm caused by the model's design, the data's bias, the threshold chosen, or the absence of human review? Courts often respond by narrowing the question. They ask whether procedures were followed. Substantive justice waits.

Ethical frameworks offer different lenses. Deontological approaches emphasise duties: if an institution deploys a system, it bears responsibility for outcomes. Consequentialist approaches weigh harms and benefits: if automation reduces overall error, some injustice may be tolerated. Virtue ethics asks a different question: what kind of institutions are we becoming when we accept harm without authorship? None of these frameworks resolves the problem alone. Together, they map its contours.

The motif threading this section is the ledger again, now with signatures missing. Transactions are recorded. Decisions logged. Yet the space for a name remains blank. In older bureaucracies, files bore stamps and initials. Errors could be traced. Apologies could be issued. In automated systems, logs replace signatures. The ledger records activity, not accountability.

Visible behaviours reveal the shift. When a wrongful denial occurs, the response is often procedural. Forms are filed. Timelines extend. The abstraction "appeal" becomes a process measured in weeks. The human cost is measured in rent arrears, stress, and stigma. Efficiency gains upstream translate into suffering downstream.

A credible limitation must be acknowledged. Single-author accountability was never universal. Large organisations have long diffused responsibility. Committees decide. Policies constrain discretion. Automation did not invent bureaucracy. The reconciliation lies in recognising that automation intensifies the diffusion while removing the interpersonal correctives that once softened it. Face-to-face encounters allowed for mercy. Systems do not blush.

Some responses aim to reintroduce authorship indirectly. Algorithmic impact assessments require institutions to anticipate harms before deployment. Audits examine outcomes after the fact. In 2019, New York City's Automated Decision Systems Task Force explored oversight mechanisms for municipal algorithms. Show the behaviour: reports commissioned. Name the abstraction: governance. Explain the mechanism: institutional checks substitute for personal responsibility. Implication: accountability becomes collective and procedural.

There are limits to this approach. Collective responsibility can become collective evasion. When everyone is responsible, no one answers. The challenge is to design systems where responsibility attaches at multiple points without evaporating. This may require assigning named stewards for systems, empowered to pause deployment and respond to harm. It may require preserving human review at critical junctures. These are design choices, not inevitabilities.

Spiritual traditions offer a parallel worth handling carefully. Confession emerged where harm exceeded individual intention. Communities developed rituals to acknowledge wrongdoing even when causation was complex. The aim was restoration rather than blame alone. The analogy suggests a posture rather than a policy. Admit harm. Repair it. Change practice. Refuse to hide behind inevitability.

The abstraction "trust" becomes visible again. People trust institutions that acknowledge error and offer redress. They withdraw trust when institutions deflect. In Michigan, trust eroded not only because the system erred, but because claimants were treated as data points rather than persons. The eventual settlements did not erase years of hardship.

A counter-example tempers despair. In some healthcare settings, algorithmic tools are deployed with explicit accountability chains. Clinicians remain responsible for decisions, using models as aids rather than authorities. Morbidity and mortality reviews examine failures openly. Show the behaviour: cases discussed. Name the abstraction: professional judgement. Explain the mechanism: human authority retained. Implication: accountability survives alongside automation.

The unresolved tension remains. As decisions become more distributed, who must answer when harm occurs? The forward test is practical. When a system denies a service wrongly, does someone step forward to say *this was our decision*, and to make amends? Or does responsibility dissolve into architecture, leaving those harmed to argue with forms and deadlines? The answer will shape whether algorithmic power is merely efficient—or morally bearable.

Chapter 4
The Personalised Self

On an evening in November 2016, millions of people refreshed their screens and found that the world appeared to agree with them. News stories aligned neatly with prior convictions. Commentators echoed familiar tones. Outrage felt justified, affirmation abundant. Only later did many realise that others, a few streets or clicks away, had been shown an entirely different account of the same events. The divergence was not the product of censorship. It was the result of personalisation doing exactly what it promised.

The paradox is sharp. Systems designed to treat each person as unique often end by making each person more predictable. They learn what holds attention, then return it in refined form. Over time, preference is mistaken for essence. A history of clicks hardens into a portrait of the self. The portrait feels intimate because it is detailed. It feels authoritative because it is persistent. It follows.

This chapter enters that intimacy with care. It asks how personalisation reshapes the experience of being a self at all. Not the abstract self of philosophy, but the everyday self who reads, watches, searches, hesitates, and wonders. The claim is not that personalisation is deceptive. It is that it is formative. It trains attention. It rewards certain desires. It quietens others. In doing so, it participates in a long conversation about identity, freedom, and the meaning of being known.

Personalisation begins innocently. Recommendation engines promise relevance. They spare us the noise of abundance. They notice what we linger on and infer what we might want next. The technique is elegant. Portraits are assembled from fragments: a watch time here, a pause there, a late-night search, a skipped article. Each fragment is trivial. Together they become consequential.

The chapter opens by examining how these portraits are built and how they change the terrain of choice. Political content offers a clear example. When feeds prioritise material likely to engage, they often amplify what provokes emotion. Over time, a user's informational environment narrows. Opposing views appear less often, not because they are banned, but because they are less likely to be clicked. Perspective shrinks without instruction. Identity feels confirmed.

This narrowing has psychological effects. When preferences are constantly mirrored back, they begin to feel fixed. Curiosity gives way to confirmation. The self is no longer something to be discovered but something to be optimised. Here the language of faith traditions becomes unexpectedly relevant. Many of them warn against confusing habit with calling, appetite with purpose. They insist that identity emerges through seeking rather than settling.

The next movement of the chapter turns to the feed itself. Curated feeds blur the line between discovery and design. Auto-play replaces wandering. Infinite scroll removes the moment of stopping. Convenience becomes the dominant virtue. The cost is subtle. When everything arrives tailored, the discipline of seeking atrophies. Surprise becomes rare, and with it the possibility of being changed by what one did not choose.

A simple contrast makes this tangible. Stumbling upon an unexpected book in a second-hand shop requires patience, attention, and openness to disappointment. An auto-play video requires none of these. Both deliver content. Only one cultivates receptivity. Spiritual traditions have long prized the former posture. Seeking was understood as a practice that formed the soul. Settling was treated with suspicion.

The chapter then turns inward, to the emotional texture of personalisation. Being mirrored constantly can feel comforting. The system appears to know what we want before we articulate it. For some, this resembles care. For others, it resembles surveillance. The same mechanism produces opposite feelings. The difference often lies in whether the mirroring feels chosen or imposed.

This ambivalence echoes older ideas of divine attention. To be seen by God was, in many traditions, a source of solace and accountability. It promised that no part of life was insignificant. At the same time, divine omniscience could unsettle. Nothing was hidden. Confession emerged as a way to navigate this tension, transforming exposure into relationship. Search histories offer no such transformation. They record without listening.

The comparison is not meant to sanctify technology or trivialise faith. It is meant to surface a question about what kind of attention forms us. Attention that invites response differs from attention that accumulates data. One addresses a person. The other profiles a user. When personalisation replaces dialogue with prediction, the self that emerges is thinner.

The chapter's final movement asks what might be recovered. If personalisation narrows, can it be interrupted? If feeds settle us, can seeking be relearned? The aim is not resistance for its own sake, but agency. A simple exercise in disrupting one's own feed serves as a prompt rather than a prescription. It creates space for surprise. Surprise, in many faiths, is where grace enters.

Throughout, the chapter returns to a recurring image: the mirror. Mirrors can clarify or distort. They can reveal or trap. A mirror that changes with every movement invites play. A mirror that freezes a moment claims truth. Personalisation tends toward the latter. It stabilises an image of the self and serves it back until it feels inevitable.

The stakes are not merely cultural. They are personal. If the self is increasingly assembled by systems that learn from past behaviour, the possibility of becoming other than one has been diminishes. Growth requires friction. Conversion requires interruption. Creativity requires the unfamiliar. A personalised environment can support these, but only if it is designed to do so.

This chapter does not argue for abandoning personalisation. It asks what kind of self it is cultivating. Are we authors of our lives, respondents to prompts, or data shadows trailing behind our past actions? The answer is not given. It is enacted, daily, in small choices about what we attend to and what we allow to surprise us.

As the chapter unfolds, readers are invited to notice their own reflections in the glass. Not to judge them, but to question them. The personalised self feels comfortable. Comfort is not the same as freedom. The pages that follow explore that difference, and the possibility that grace may still arrive from outside the feed, unannounced, asking to be noticed.

Portraits Built from Clicks

In November 2016, in Menlo Park, California, engineers at Facebook confronted an uncomfortable public reckoning. In the weeks following the US presidential election, journalists and researchers showed that users had been exposed to sharply different political news feeds, often reinforcing existing views. The company acknowledged that its ranking systems prioritised engagement—likes, shares, watch time—over balance. The outcome was not censorship. It was segmentation. The feed had learned what each person lingered on and gave them more of it.

Five words belong here. *Clicks became convictions.*

Personalisation begins as a promise of care. It offers relevance in a world of excess. It spares attention. It learns from behaviour and adapts. The machinery is subtle. Each interaction—scrolling past, pausing, sharing—adds a brushstroke to a portrait. Over time, the portrait acquires depth and confidence. It claims to represent who someone *is*, not merely what they have done.

The portrait is built from fragments. Recommendation engines do not ask people who they are. They infer. They measure dwell time rather than belief, repetition rather than reflection. A preference is registered when a video plays to completion. A leaning is inferred when a link is shared. Trust, an abstraction, becomes a metric: engagement rate. Identity becomes a cluster of signals. The implication is quiet but profound. Behaviour becomes destiny's raw material.

Political content illustrates the process starkly. In 2015 and 2016, researchers at MIT and elsewhere observed that false or emotionally charged news spread more rapidly on social platforms than sober reporting (Vosoughi, Roy, and Aral, *Science*, 2018). Show the behaviour: users share content that provokes outrage. Name the abstraction: relevance. Explain the mechanism: ranking systems reward engagement. Implication: feeds tilt toward material that confirms and inflames.

Once a feed learns a pattern, it optimises around it. A user who watches a few partisan videos is shown more from similar sources. Alternative perspectives appear less often, not because they are suppressed, but because they perform poorly against the system's objectives. The portrait sharpens. The mirror stiffens.

The quiet motif threading this process is the portrait itself. Portraits select. They frame. They omit. A painter chooses light and shadow. A recommender chooses signals. Neither is neutral. The difference is scale. Millions of portraits are updated continuously, each claiming intimacy without relationship.

Preferences harden into identities through repetition. What begins as curiosity becomes habit. Habit becomes expectation. Expectation becomes self-description. *This is the kind of person I am.* The system did not command this conclusion. It suggested it, repeatedly. The visible behaviour—clicking what feels familiar—reinforces the inference. The abstraction "choice" narrows into routine.

A second named example deepens the picture. In 2019, YouTube adjusted its recommendation algorithms to reduce the spread of borderline political content, following criticism that its autoplay feature nudged users toward increasingly extreme material. The company reported reductions in watch time for such content. Show the behaviour: downranking certain videos. Name the abstraction: responsibility. Explain the mechanism: altering optimisation targets. Implication: portraits can be redrawn when values change.

This counter-example matters. Personalisation does not inevitably narrow horizons. It does so when systems optimise for a single value, usually engagement. When designers introduce counterweights—diversity, novelty, editorial judgement—the portrait becomes less rigid. The reconciliation is design, not denial.

Yet even with safeguards, the portrait remains a simplification. It cannot see reasons. It cannot distinguish between watching out of agreement and watching out of concern. It cannot tell whether a click expresses conviction or boredom. It records action and infers essence. The risk is mistaking trace for truth.

The abstraction "efficiency" becomes visible here. A feed that learns quickly saves time. It reduces search costs. Users report satisfaction. The cost is opportunity. Discovery gives way to delivery. Seeking becomes unnecessary. Over time, curiosity dulls.

This matters beyond politics. Music, books, friendships, and faith communities are all filtered through personalised systems. A listener who enjoys a genre is served more of it. The pleasure is real. So is the narrowing. The portrait becomes a feedback device, reflecting taste until taste stabilises.

Older traditions recognised this danger in different terms. Habit could form virtue or vice. Attention shaped desire. Practices of fasting, pilgrimage, or study disrupted routine to prevent identity from calcifying. The aim was not novelty for its own sake, but openness to transformation. Personalisation tends the other way. It stabilises.

The emotional experience of the portrait oscillates between comfort and unease. Feeling recognised can feel affirming. The system seems to *get* you. At the same time, the persistence of the mirror can feel intrusive. The portrait follows across contexts. It remembers. It updates. Being seen without being heard produces a thin intimacy.

A credible limitation tempers alarm. People have always lived within informational niches. Newspapers had editorial lines. Communities shared assumptions. The difference now is permeability. Digital niches are more precise and less porous. Crossing boundaries requires effort. The default is enclosure.

Metrics make this visible. Studies of media consumption show declining overlap between audiences of opposing political outlets in the United States after 2010 (Pew Research Center, 2014). Show the behaviour: audiences cluster. Name the abstraction: polarisation. Explain the mechanism: personalised distribution. Implication: common ground thins.

The portrait also travels. Data collected in one context informs another. A search about an illness influences advertising. A viewing history influences recommendations elsewhere. The self becomes portable, compressed, and reusable. The abstraction "privacy" becomes a series of settings few revisit.

Return to the mirror. A mirror that adapts to every gesture risks trapping the subject in a loop of self-confirmation. A mirror that resists—by showing what is unfamiliar—can provoke growth. The choice between these mirrors is not technological fate. It is a design and governance question.

Some platforms experiment with disruption. News apps introduce "opposing views" features. Music services inject randomness. These are modest interventions. They acknowledge a truth long known in spiritual practice: surprise matters. It breaks the spell of habit.

The unresolved tension presses forward. Personalisation promises to honour individuality. It often delivers predictability instead. The forward test is intimate. When a feed reflects you perfectly, does it leave room for who you might become?

Curated Feeds and the Loss of Seeking

In July 2013, in Mountain View, California, Google announced a change that passed with little public ceremony. Autoplay would become the default behaviour for YouTube recommendations on many devices. The platform's engineers reported that continuous playback increased watch time and user satisfaction. Videos would no longer end cleanly. They would *continue.* What followed was not outrage, but acquiescence. Discovery became frictionless. Stopping required effort.

Five words belong here. *The search quietly disappeared.*

Curated feeds promise relief from excess. They step in where abundance overwhelms. Instead of asking, they offer. Instead of waiting, they deliver. The design is persuasive because it feels helpful. Why search when what you want appears before you know you want it? Yet this convenience alters the posture of the mind. Seeking gives way to receiving. Curiosity is satisfied before it stretches.

The distinction matters. Seeking is an active stance. It involves uncertainty, disappointment, and risk. It requires attention directed outward rather than held in place. Curated feeds reverse this dynamic. They anticipate desire based on past behaviour and remove the need to ask. The abstraction "efficiency" becomes a behaviour: accepting the next item without pause. The implication is subtle. When the path is smoothed, wandering becomes unnecessary.

A simple contrast brings the difference into focus. Consider stumbling upon an unexpected book in a second-hand shop. The experience begins with not knowing. Shelves are uneven. Titles compete for attention. A spine catches the eye for reasons that are difficult to articulate. The book may disappoint. It may linger for years. The cost is time. The reward is surprise.

Now consider an auto-play video. It begins immediately. The choice has already been made. The system inferred interest from prior views. There is no disappointment because expectation is managed. There is also little surprise. The next item resembles the last. The visible metric—completion rate—confirms success. Curiosity is unnecessary. Satisfaction is brief.

Curated feeds blur the line between discovery and design. Discovery suggests encounter. Design suggests intention. When feeds curate relentlessly, encounters are engineered. The user feels agency because content aligns with preference. The system feels invisible because its hand is gentle. Over time, the distinction erodes. What appears is mistaken for what exists.

This erosion has cognitive consequences. Research in psychology and media studies has shown that exploratory behaviour declines when options are pre-ranked. A 2018 study by Menczer and Hills on information foraging observed that users presented with ranked lists were less likely to explore beyond the first few items. Show the behaviour: clicking top results. Name the abstraction: convenience. Explain the mechanism: reduced search cost biases selection. Implication: horizons narrow without awareness.

Spiritual traditions recognised a version of this danger long before algorithms. Seeking was treated as formative. In the Christian gospels, seeking precedes finding. In Jewish tradition, study is valued precisely because it resists closure. In Sufism, the seeker is praised for restlessness, not certainty. The shared intuition is that meaning emerges through pursuit rather than possession.

Settling too quickly was treated with suspicion. Comfort could harden into complacency. Practices such as pilgrimage, fasting, and retreat disrupted routine to renew attention. These practices were inefficient by design. They created space for questions to outlast answers. Curated feeds do the opposite. They resolve questions instantly.

The abstraction "trust" becomes visible here. Users trust feeds to surface what matters. The feed earns that trust by performing reliably. Each relevant suggestion reinforces confidence. Over time, trust transfers from one's own seeking capacity to the system's anticipatory power. The implication is not dependence in the crude sense, but delegation of curiosity.

A second named example sharpens the concern. In 2020, Netflix disclosed that over 80 per cent of viewing on the platform was driven by recommendations rather than deliberate search. Show the behaviour: viewers accept suggestions. Name the abstraction: satisfaction. Explain the mechanism: predictive ranking reduces choice fatigue. Implication: serendipity declines as selection is automated.

There is a credible counter-example worth holding. Curated systems can expose users to material they would never have sought intentionally. Music recommendation engines have introduced listeners to new genres and artists. The reconciliation lies in intent. When systems are designed to balance familiarity with novelty, they can support discovery. When they optimise solely for retention, they tend to repeat.

The quiet motif threading this section is the path. Seeking involves choosing paths without maps. Curated feeds pave the path in advance. Walking becomes easier. Orientation becomes unnecessary. Over time, the muscles for wandering weaken.

The loss of seeking also affects patience. When answers arrive instantly, questions shorten. Reflection compresses. The abstraction "attention" becomes a behaviour: skimming rather than dwelling. This matters for moral and spiritual life, where depth often requires delay. Many traditions insisted on waiting precisely because insight could not be rushed.

Curated feeds also reshape memory. When content flows endlessly, nothing needs to be remembered. The feed remembers for you. This externalisation of memory alters how experiences integrate. A book discovered by chance often carries a story of how it was found. An auto-play video leaves little trace once it ends. The self accumulates consumption without narrative.

The design of feeds reinforces this. Infinite scroll removes natural stopping points. Auto-play eliminates silence. The system measures success by continuity. Stopping looks like failure. The abstraction "engagement" becomes a behaviour: staying longer than intended. The implication is not addiction in the clinical sense, but enclosure of attention.

Spiritual disciplines often inserted stops deliberately. Bells marked hours. Sabbaths interrupted work. Fasts created hunger. These interruptions were not punitive. They restored proportion. Curated feeds resist interruption. They flow.

Some platforms have begun to experiment with friction. Reminders to take breaks. Options to disable auto-play. These gestures acknowledge a truth the past articulated clearly: seeking requires space. Without space, desire loops.

Return to the bookshop. The unexpected book required effort to find and effort to carry. It may have changed how one thought. Or it may have bored. Both outcomes mattered. Seeking accepts risk. Curated feeds minimise it.

The unresolved tension presses forward. If convenience continues to replace seeking, what capacities are we relinquishing? The forward test is modest and immediate. When the next item appears without being asked for, will it be accepted—or will the pause be reclaimed, long enough to ask what might be found by searching instead?

Feeling Known, Feeling Watched

In June 2013, in Hong Kong, Edward Snowden met journalists from *The Guardian* and disclosed the existence of the US National Security Agency's PRISM programme. The documents showed how major technology companies, including Google, were compelled to provide access to user data under secret court orders. The revelation triggered global debate. People did not discover that data was collected; many had assumed that already. They discovered how *completely* it could be seen.

Five words belong here. *Someone was always paying attention.*

That attention sits at the centre of a modern emotional paradox. The same systems that unsettle by their watchfulness also comfort by their recognition. A search engine that finishes a question before it is typed can feel uncannily attuned. A streaming service that knows what suits a quiet evening can feel considerate. Being mirrored by machines oscillates between intimacy and intrusion. The difference is rarely technical. It is relational.

To feel known is a human longing. Infants thrive when attention is consistent. Adults ache to be recognised without having to explain themselves. Personalised systems tap into this longing by reflecting patterns back to users with precision. The abstraction "care" becomes a behaviour: relevant results appear quickly. The abstraction "understanding" becomes a metric: reduced friction. The implication is warmth without reciprocity.

Yet the same mirror can chill. When the reflection persists across contexts—work, home, leisure—it begins to feel like surveillance. The abstraction "efficiency" becomes a behaviour: tracking across platforms. The implication is exposure without consent. Feeling known tips into feeling watched when attention is continuous, asymmetric, and unanswerable.

This ambivalence is not new. Religious traditions wrestled with it long before data centres existed. Divine attention was described as total. Nothing hidden. Every hair counted. For some, this was consolation. For others, it provoked fear. The difference lay in character. Was the one who saw also the one who listened? Was attention paired with mercy?

Confession offers a revealing comparison. In many Christian traditions, confession is a voluntary act. The penitent chooses disclosure. Speech is offered, not extracted. The confessor listens, responds, and keeps silence beyond the ritual. The purpose is restoration, not record-keeping. Memory serves forgiveness.

Now compare a search history. Queries accumulate automatically. No intention to disclose is required. The system records curiosity, fear, boredom, and desire without context. There is no response, only retention. Memory serves optimisation. The visible behaviour—typing late-night questions—becomes data. The abstraction "self-knowledge" is replaced by profiling.

The emotional difference is stark. Confession risks shame but promises relief. Search histories promise convenience but risk unease. One involves agency. The other operates by default. The same content—questions never asked aloud—moves through entirely different moral architectures.

A second named example sharpens the contrast. In 2018, Cambridge Analytica's use of Facebook data revealed how personal information, gathered under the guise of social connection, had been repurposed for political profiling. Show the outcome: public outrage, regulatory scrutiny. Name the abstraction: trust. Explain the mechanism: data collected for one relationship deployed in another. Implication: feeling known curdles into betrayal.

Trust depends on boundaries. Being seen within agreed limits builds intimacy. Being seen without limit erodes it. Personalised systems often blur these boundaries by design. Data flows across contexts invisibly. A purchase influences an advert. A search influences a feed. The user experiences coherence. The system experiences continuity. The difference matters.

The quiet motif threading this section is the gaze. Who looks, for how long, and with what intention? In art, a gaze can dignify or dominate. In technology, the gaze is automated and persistent. It does not avert its eyes. It does not tire. It does not forget.

Psychological research helps clarify the impact. Studies on surveillance show that perceived observation alters behaviour, even when no action follows. People self-censor. Risk-taking declines. Conformity increases. Show the behaviour: users avoid searching certain topics. Name the abstraction: freedom. Explain the mechanism: anticipation of judgement shapes action. Implication: possibility contracts.

At the same time, personalisation can reduce loneliness. Recommendation systems surface communities of shared interest. People feel less isolated when content resonates. The counter-example matters. Not all attention wounds. The reconciliation lies in symmetry. Attention that can be questioned, reciprocated, or withdrawn feels different from attention that cannot.

Divine attention, at its best, was imagined as symmetrical in a moral sense. Humans could protest, lament, argue. Sacred texts preserve these exchanges. Surveillance systems offer no such dialogue. Appeals are procedural, not relational. The abstraction "accountability" becomes a ticket number.

The metric of being watched is not only data volume. It is persistence. Systems remember what humans would forget. A momentary curiosity becomes a lasting signal. The implication is temporal. Past selves linger. The possibility of reinvention thins.

Some platforms attempt to soften this by offering controls: history deletion, private modes. These gestures acknowledge unease. They also place the burden on users to manage attention asymmetries they did not design. The abstraction "consent" becomes a settings menu few revisit.

The spiritual comparison must be handled carefully. Equating algorithms with God trivialises both. The point is not identity but contrast. Divine attention was framed as purposeful, personal, and oriented toward good. Algorithmic attention is instrumental, impersonal, and oriented toward prediction. Confusing the two leads to misplaced trust or misplaced fear.

Return to the mirror. A mirror held briefly can reassure. A mirror fixed to the wall, recording every movement, alters how one lives. The difference is duration and intent. Feeling known requires the possibility of turning away.

The unresolved tension presses forward. As systems continue to mirror us with increasing fidelity, will that attention be shaped to invite response—or will it remain a silent gaze? The next time a system anticipates a desire before it is spoken, the question is not whether it is accurate. It is whether being seen still feels like recognition, or whether it has crossed into watchfulness that no longer asks permission.

Recovering Surprise and Grace

On 12 March 2009, in Pasadena, California, a researcher named Eli Pariser stood on a TED stage and described what he called the "filter bubble". He argued that personalisation systems were quietly shaping what people saw, narrowing their informational worlds without consent or awareness. The talk travelled widely. It offered a language for a sensation many already had: the strange comfort of being perfectly catered to, paired with the dullness of never being startled. Pariser's phrase stuck because it named a loss that rarely shows up in analytics.

Five words matter here. *Nothing unexpected found its way.*

Surprise is not a luxury. It is a condition of growth. Without it, learning becomes repetition and identity becomes rehearsal. Personalisation is often praised for reducing friction: fewer irrelevant results, fewer wasted minutes, more "you" in what you see. Yet friction sometimes protects the self from becoming a closed loop. A life without surprise is efficient, and small.

The question at the end of this chapter is therefore not merely about technology. It is about the kind of person formed by constant mirroring. A personalised environment invites the self to become an echo of its past behaviour. It trains attention toward what already pleases. It rewards the familiar. Over time, the self begins to resemble its data trail: coherent, predictable, and thin.

Three figures help name the drift. The author chooses, revises, and resists. The respondent answers prompts presented by others. The data shadow trails behind, made from traces, consulted by systems, and treated as the self's most reliable version. Most people live among all three. The danger is not that the shadow exists, but that it starts to speak with the author's voice.

Show the behaviour. A person opens a news app and reads only what appears at the top. A playlist runs without interruption. A feed supplies opinions that feel instantly intelligible. Name the abstraction: agency. Explain the mechanism: ranking systems reward quick engagement and return similar material. Implication: the user becomes a respondent, not because choice disappears, but because the environment presents choices already shaped.

To talk about grace in this context requires care. Grace, in many traditions, is not merely kindness. It is interruption. It is the arrival of what one did not earn or predict, a gift that unsettles entitlement and enlarges possibility. In Christian theology, grace breaks the logic of merit. In Jewish narratives, blessing arrives through unlikely routes. In Islamic thought, guidance is received, not manufactured. In Buddhist practice, awakening comes when habitual grasping loosens. Across these frameworks, what matters is not surprise as entertainment, but surprise as transformation.

Personalisation is not hostile to transformation, but it does not naturally cultivate it. Its logic is reinforcement. A system that learns from past behaviour tends to offer more of what past behaviour suggests will be accepted. That is its purpose. The abstraction "relevance" becomes a metric: click-through rate. The abstraction "satisfaction" becomes a behaviour: longer sessions. Implication: disruption looks like failure.

This has cultural consequences. When information environments narrow, public life loses shared reference points. When entertainment becomes perfectly tailored, collective imagination fragments. When identities are continually affirmed, the capacity to be corrected declines. Surprise is how correction arrives without violence. It introduces a pause between the self's certainty and the world's complexity.

A second named example clarifies the stakes. In 2018, researchers at MIT published findings in *Science* showing that false news spread faster and farther on Twitter than true news, partly because novelty drives sharing (Vosoughi, Roy, and Aral, 2018). Novelty, in other words, is powerful. It can enlighten or mislead. The reconciliation is important. Seeking surprise is not the same as chasing novelty. Systems that maximise novelty may increase misinformation. Systems that suppress novelty may increase complacency. The question is not whether surprise is good. It is what kind of surprise forms wisdom rather than mania.

The motif threading this section is the open door. Personalisation closes doors gently, by making certain paths easier than others. Grace, in many stories, arrives as a door unexpectedly opening—an encounter, a text, a sentence overheard, a friendship formed outside one's pattern. The problem is not that personalisation shuts every door. It is that it teaches people to stop looking for them.

Recovering surprise begins with recognising that seeking is a practice, not a mood. It requires small acts of deliberate misalignment with one's own patterns. This can be done without drama. The aim is not to reject curated systems entirely, but to interrupt their authority over what counts as relevant.

Here a simple exercise becomes useful, not as advice but as a diagnostic. For one week, choose one daily moment of media consumption—ten minutes is enough—and refuse personalisation. Use a private browsing mode for a single search. Read a newspaper section you never choose. Watch a lecture on a subject outside your field. Listen to a genre you have previously dismissed. The visible behaviour is modest. The effect is revealing. You begin to notice how quickly the mind asks to return to familiar comfort. You feel the pull of the feed.

Another variation is even simpler. Before clicking the first recommended item, pause and ask what the system thinks you are. Not what you think you are. What your patterns have told it. The abstraction "identity" becomes visible in the recommendation itself. The implication is clarifying. If the system's portrait feels too accurate, it may also be too narrow.

A credible limitation must be faced. Many people rely on personalisation for accessibility and connection. Disabled users benefit from adaptive interfaces. Isolated individuals find communities through recommendation systems. Parents with little time need efficiency. Surprise cannot become a privilege reserved for those with leisure. The reconciliation lies in proportionality. The point is not constant disruption, but intentional openings—small windows in which the self can encounter what it did not pre-select.

Faith traditions offer language for this proportionality. The sabbath interrupts labour without abolishing it. Fasting interrupts eating without condemning it. Pilgrimage interrupts routine without making home meaningless. These practices assume that interruption restores rather than destroys. They treat habit as necessary but dangerous when unchecked.

The emotional experience of this recovery can be strange. At first, the unfamiliar feels irrelevant. That is the point. Personalisation trains the self to equate relevance with comfort. Seeking trains the self to tolerate the unfamiliar long enough for meaning to emerge. The visible metric is not engagement time. It is attention held in uncertainty.

The question of authorship returns here. An author does not merely express preferences. An author chooses what to dwell on, what to resist, and what to revise. A respondent accepts prompts. A data shadow accumulates traces. The exercise of disruption is a small act of authorship. It asserts that the self is not reducible to its past clicks.

Grace, in this framing, is not something a system can deliver on demand. That is precisely why it matters. It arrives from outside the optimised loop. It may arrive through a book stumbled upon, a conversation overheard, a piece of art that unsettles rather than pleases. It may arrive through an algorithmic recommendation that unexpectedly breaks pattern, but only if the system is designed to allow it and the user is willing to receive it. The point is not to romanticise randomness. It is to refuse enclosure.

The unresolved tension remains. As personalisation grows more precise, will surprise become a rare accident—or a chosen discipline? The next time a feed offers the perfect next item, the forward test is quiet but decisive: will you accept the mirror as the whole self, or will you open a door the system did not think to show you?

Chapter 5
Prediction, Risk, and Surrender

On the morning of 29 October 2012, residents of New York City watched a weather map more closely than they watched the sky. Hurricane Sandy was approaching, and the forecasts were unusually confident. Coloured cones tightened. Probability bands narrowed. City officials ordered evacuations, transit systems shut down, and hospitals moved patients pre-emptively. When the storm arrived, it confounded some expectations and confirmed others. The city flooded in places that had not flooded before. In others, the water stopped just short. Afterwards, the conversation turned quickly from survival to prediction: why had some models missed, while others came so close?

What was striking was not the reliance on forecasts—that reliance was justified—but the emotional texture of the reliance. People spoke as if the future had briefly become legible, then betrayed them. The language of chance carried moral weight. Accuracy felt like virtue. Error felt like failure.

Prediction has become one of the defining gestures of modern life. We forecast weather, markets, disease, traffic, crime, and personal compatibility. We assign scores to creditworthiness, insurance risk, academic potential, and health outcomes. These numbers promise clarity. They tame uncertainty by translating it into probability, and probability into action. Much of this is an unambiguous good. Forecasts save lives. Risk models allocate scarce resources. Planning becomes possible where fatalism once ruled.

Yet something else happens alongside these gains. As prediction becomes more precise and pervasive, uncertainty begins to look like a problem to be eliminated rather than a condition to be inhabited. Not knowing comes to feel irresponsible. Hesitation looks like ignorance. The future, once approached with humility or hope, is increasingly treated as a technical challenge. This chapter examines what is gained—and what is quietly lost—when uncertainty is framed almost entirely as risk to be managed.

The opening movement of the chapter surveys the spread of predictive tools across everyday life. Finance was an early adopter, turning volatility into models and derivatives. Health care followed, using risk scores to identify patients most likely to deteriorate. Even mundane planning now leans heavily on prediction: navigation apps estimate arrival times to the minute, productivity software forecasts task completion, dating platforms score compatibility. The example of weather apps offers a telling contrast. Once, people read the sky, listened to elders, or accepted surprise. Now, a precise percentage chance of rain sets expectations. When the rain fails to arrive, disappointment follows. The forecast, not the sky, has become the reference point.

The chapter does not dismiss these tools. It treats them with respect. Prediction, when used well, is a form of care. It allows preparation. It reduces harm. The danger lies not in prediction itself, but in its quiet expansion from aid to authority. When numbers become the primary way of relating to the future, they begin to shape imagination. The future looks narrower, more settled, even before it arrives.

From here, the chapter turns to an older register of human response: the spiritual role of not knowing. Across traditions, uncertainty was not merely endured; it was cultivated. Not knowing drove prayer, fasting, consultation, and collective vigilance. Vulnerability was shared rather than outsourced to experts. A looming threat—a drought, a plague, a war—often elicited communal rituals that acknowledged dependence and limited control. These practices did not produce predictions. They produced solidarity.

This section asks an uncomfortable question. When uncertainty is reframed entirely as calculable risk, what happens to humility? What happens to trust that is not anchored in forecasts? Some forms of trust require exposure. They assume that not everything can be secured in advance. Spiritual traditions often insisted that such exposure was formative. It taught restraint, patience, and mutual care. Prediction can reduce exposure so effectively that these capacities atrophy.

The next movement of the chapter addresses a subtle shift in public language. Probability increasingly functions like fate. Phrases such as "it was inevitable" or "the data showed it would happen" appear after events, lending them an air of necessity. High likelihood slides into moral permission. If an outcome is probable, resistance can seem futile or even foolish. This drift is especially visible in debates about predictive policing and risk assessment in criminal justice, where statistical correlations are sometimes treated as destiny rather than tendency.

The chapter challenges this slippage without caricature. Probability describes patterns, not obligations. A forecast does not absolve responsibility. Treating likelihood as fate collapses the space for judgement. It replaces discernment with resignation. Here the book's broader themes resurface. When systems appear to know the future, human agency feels redundant. Faith, whether religious or secular, begins to migrate from character and choice to models and metrics.

The closing movement sketches an alternative stance, neither anti-prediction nor submissive to it. The aim is to live informed but not ruled. This posture recognises the value of forecasts while refusing to let them dominate moral imagination. It resembles a tension long articulated in spiritual teaching: effort without illusion of control, surrender without passivity. One plans carefully, then holds plans lightly. One prepares for likely outcomes without treating them as decrees.

A brief reflection at the end of the chapter invites readers to notice where prediction exerts disproportionate authority in their own lives. Not to reject it, but to rebalance it. To ask where numbers have crowded out judgement, or where risk management has displaced trust. The question is not whether to forecast, but how to remain human in the presence of forecasts.

Prediction promises mastery. Surrender sounds like its opposite. This chapter argues that they are not enemies. When rightly ordered, they belong together. The pages that follow explore how numbers can inform action without becoming idols, and how letting go of total control may be the most responsible response to a future that remains, despite all models, unfinished.

Taming Uncertainty with Numbers

In September 1987, in Reading, England, the European Centre for Medium-Range Weather Forecasts issued a forecast that many British meteorologists dismissed. Its model suggested a violent storm would hit southern England on the night of 15 October. The UK Met Office, relying on different assumptions and sparse data, downplayed the risk. The storm arrived with ferocity, killing eighteen people and felling millions of trees. Afterwards, the episode became a turning point. Numerical weather prediction gained authority. The sky had spoken. The numbers spoke louder.

Five words belong here. *The map replaced the clouds.*

Prediction has always existed. What changed in the late twentieth century was its scale, speed, and social prestige. Uncertainty, once treated as an inescapable feature of life, began to look like a technical problem awaiting better tools. Forecasting models improved. Data streams multiplied. Computation accelerated. Numbers promised to domesticate chance.

The appeal is obvious. Prediction markets aggregate dispersed knowledge. Risk scores summarise complex histories into actionable signals. Forecasting tools allow planning across time horizons once ruled by guesswork. In finance, volatility can be priced. In health, probabilities can guide prevention. In daily life, navigation apps estimate arrival times to the minute. The abstraction "control" becomes visible as a behaviour: acting earlier, with greater confidence.

Finance offers an early and influential example. In the 1970s, the Black–Scholes model transformed options trading by translating uncertainty into calculable risk. Traders could price derivatives using inputs such as volatility and time to expiry. Show the behaviour: widespread adoption on trading floors. Name the abstraction: risk management. Explain the mechanism: probabilistic models reduce ambiguity to price. Implication: markets expand as uncertainty becomes tradable.

The benefits were real. Liquidity increased. Hedging became possible. At the same time, the seduction was subtle. When models worked well, they invited trust beyond their assumptions. Rare events were discounted because they sat outside historical data. The 2008 financial crisis exposed this limitation brutally. Models had tamed familiar uncertainty while amplifying unfamiliar risk. The reconciliation is instructive. Numbers did not fail because they existed. They failed because they were treated as exhaustive.

Health care provides a second, quieter illustration. Risk scores such as the Framingham Risk Score, developed in Massachusetts in the 1950s and refined over decades, estimate an individual's likelihood of developing cardiovascular disease. Show the behaviour: clinicians use scores to guide treatment thresholds. Name the abstraction: prevention. Explain the mechanism: population data informs individual probability. Implication: earlier intervention saves lives.

Here again, the benefits are substantial. Preventive medicine depends on forecasting. Yet the seduction persists. A risk score can begin to stand in for a person. Lifestyle, context, and values recede behind a percentage. Patients may hear a number as destiny rather than tendency. The abstraction "likelihood" hardens into expectation.

Everyday planning now leans heavily on similar tools. Weather apps exemplify the shift. Before numerical models, people read the sky, noted wind direction, listened to local knowledge. Expectation was elastic. Rain might come. It might not. Today, an app announces a 70 per cent chance of rain at 3 p.m. The forecast does not merely inform. It sets a standard against which reality is judged. When rain fails to appear, disappointment follows. The sky has not lied. The model feels as though it has.

This change in expectation matters. A forecast reframes uncertainty as error rather than mystery. The abstraction "accuracy" becomes a behaviour: refreshing the app. The implication is psychological. Not knowing feels less tolerable when numbers promise to know better.

Prediction markets extend the logic further. Platforms such as the Iowa Electronic Markets, established in 1988, have often outperformed polls in forecasting election outcomes. Show the behaviour: participants trade contracts tied to future events. Name the abstraction: collective intelligence. Explain the mechanism: prices aggregate beliefs. Implication: uncertainty appears to dissolve into consensus.

The success of such markets fuels a broader faith in prediction. If enough data and incentives align, the future seems legible. Yet even here, limitations persist. Markets predict outcomes, not meanings. They cannot tell whether an outcome is just, only whether it is likely. Confusing the two invites moral abdication.

The quiet motif threading this section is the net. Numbers cast a net over the future, catching patterns and probabilities. A finer net catches more detail. It also gives the illusion that nothing escapes. What slips through—novelty, rupture, grace—becomes harder to name.

A credible counter-example tempers the narrative. Some uncertainties resist quantification productively. In creative work, over-forecasting can stifle innovation. In relationships, excessive risk calculation can paralyse commitment. The reconciliation lies in domain sensitivity. Prediction excels where patterns repeat. It falters where meaning emerges from singular encounters.

The abstraction "trust" becomes visible here. Trust in numbers grows when forecasts succeed. It shifts authority from judgement to models. This shift can be prudent. It can also narrow responsibility. When a decision is justified by a score, dissent appears irrational. The implication is institutional. Organisations begin to hide behind metrics.

Weather forecasting again offers insight. Modern models, including those run by the ECMWF, have dramatically improved accuracy over the past four decades. Five-day forecasts now rival two-day forecasts from the 1980s. Show the behaviour: governments rely on early warnings. Name the abstraction: preparedness. Explain the mechanism: ensemble modelling captures uncertainty ranges. Implication: harm is reduced.

At the same time, meteorologists now speak carefully about probabilities, emphasising uncertainty bands rather than single outcomes. This is not weakness. It is epistemic humility encoded in practice. Where such humility is lost, numbers become idols.

Old sky-reading habits were not scientific in the modern sense, but they carried an implicit wisdom. They acknowledged limits. They treated the future as responsive, not fixed. People prepared, but they also waited. The posture was different. Expectation remained open.

The seduction of numbers lies in their clarity. A percentage feels solid. It invites action. It quiets anxiety. Yet clarity can overreach. When everything is framed as manageable risk, vulnerability appears as failure rather than condition. The abstraction "resilience" becomes a metric, stripped of its relational roots.

The forward tension presses. As prediction tools spread further into daily life, what stance toward uncertainty will prevail? Will numbers remain guides, or will they become governors? The next chapter asks how not knowing once shaped humility and solidarity. The question left hanging here is simpler and sharper. When the forecast is always at hand, will there still be room to look up at the sky—and accept that some clouds cannot be calculated away?

The Spiritual Role of Not Knowing

In March 1348, as the Black Death reached Florence, the city's physicians disagreed about causes and cures. Some blamed corrupted air, others planetary alignment. None could predict who would fall ill next. In response, civic authorities organised processions and public prayers, while confraternities called for days of fasting. Families kept vigil through the night. Fear was shared. No one claimed mastery. The city did not know what would happen. *They waited together.*

Not knowing has always been dangerous. It exposes the limits of control and the fragility of plans. Yet across cultures, uncertainty was not treated solely as a deficit to be eliminated. It was also a summons. When outcomes could not be calculated, people turned toward practices that cultivated humility and solidarity. Prayer, fasting, lament, and watchfulness did not reduce risk in the modern sense. They reoriented response.

The abstraction "uncertainty" becomes visible here as a behaviour: gathering rather than dispersing. When outcomes could not be secured, communities tightened bonds. Vigil meant staying awake with others. Fasting meant refusing private consolation. The implication was moral. Vulnerability was not managed individually. It was borne together.

This posture contrasts sharply with a world organised around risk management. Risk promises comparability. It converts danger into gradients and thresholds. The benefits are real. In public health, risk models guide vaccination strategies. In disaster response, forecasts enable evacuation. Yet when every threat is framed as manageable risk, a different loss emerges. Not knowing becomes intolerable. Waiting looks like negligence.

Spiritual traditions often insisted on the opposite. Waiting was a discipline. In the Hebrew scriptures, watchfulness marks moments of transition: before liberation, before judgement, before renewal. The behaviour is simple: staying present without resolution. The abstraction "hope" becomes a practice rather than a prediction. The implication is patience without passivity.

A second historical example sharpens the pattern. In April 1918, as influenza spread through American cities, churches and synagogues in Philadelphia organised days of prayer and fasting even as public gatherings were later restricted. Newspapers reported queues forming outside places of worship. Show the behaviour: collective abstention and vigil. Name the abstraction: humility. Explain the mechanism: acknowledging dependence in the face of uncertainty. Implication: trust was placed not in foresight but in mutual care.

This is not nostalgia. Such practices did not stop disease. They did shape response. They discouraged scapegoating. They reminded participants that no one stood outside risk. In doing so, they tempered fear with solidarity.

Modern risk frameworks can inadvertently do the opposite. By segmenting populations into risk categories, they encourage differential treatment. This is often necessary. It can also fracture shared responsibility. When vulnerability is individualised, empathy thins. The abstraction "efficiency" becomes a behaviour: targeting interventions narrowly. The implication is social distance.

Trust depends on exposure. This claim unsettles modern sensibilities. We often imagine trust as something that follows assurance. Historically, it often preceded it. People trusted precisely because outcomes were unknown. Marriage vows, monastic commitments, and covenants were entered without actuarial tables. The behaviour was commitment without guarantee. The abstraction "faithfulness" became visible in endurance.

A credible limitation must be named. Not knowing can be weaponised. Appeals to mystery have excused negligence and abuse. When uncertainty is used to silence inquiry, humility curdles into obscurantism. The reconciliation is discernment. Spiritual traditions distinguished between mysteries that invite reverence and questions that demand investigation. Not knowing did not cancel responsibility. It located it within limits.

The quiet motif threading this section is the vigil. A vigil is neither action nor inaction. It is presence under uncertainty. Candles burn. Time passes. People remain. The vigil refuses premature closure. It also refuses despair. In a culture of dashboards and alerts, the vigil looks inefficient. Its value lies elsewhere.

Risk language reshapes emotional life. When danger is quantified, anxiety migrates from fear of the unknown to fear of deviation from forecasts. A low probability can still terrify. A high probability can numb. The abstraction "safety" becomes a number. The implication is behavioural: refreshing updates rather than attending to neighbours.

Prayer functions differently. It does not predict. It addresses. Whether one believes it changes outcomes is secondary to how it changes posture. Prayer acknowledges that some goods cannot be secured by effort alone. It trains attention toward dependence without paralysis. In communal settings, it synchronises concern. People worry together.

Fasting intensifies this synchrony. By abstaining collectively, participants feel risk in their bodies. Hunger becomes a shared metric. The abstraction "vulnerability" becomes a sensation. The implication is empathy grounded in experience rather than calculation.

Modern systems often aim to remove such sensations. Pain is medicated. Delay is optimised away. This is humane in many contexts. It also reduces occasions for shared endurance. When suffering is privatised, solidarity weakens.

The question posed here is not whether to abandon risk management. It is what disappears when it becomes the only language available. If every uncertainty is framed as solvable, then failure feels shameful rather than tragic. If every vulnerability is preventable, then those who suffer appear culpable. The moral texture shifts.

A contemporary illustration brings this into focus. During the early months of the COVID-19 pandemic in 2020, risk models guided policy across Europe. At the same time, many communities revived older practices: balcony vigils in Italy, communal clapping in the United Kingdom, online prayer services across traditions. Show the behaviour: synchronised acts without instrumental payoff. Name the abstraction: solidarity. Explain the mechanism: shared ritual under uncertainty. Implication: trust was rebuilt horizontally when vertical control faltered.

Here the reconciliation appears. Prediction and prayer addressed different needs. Models informed decisions. Rituals sustained morale. Where either tried to replace the other, distortions followed. Where they coexisted, response proved more resilient.

The spiritual role of not knowing also disciplines speech. It restrains certainty. In traditions of lament, complaints are voiced without solutions. Words are offered to name pain rather than to close it. The abstraction "truth" becomes honesty about limits. The implication is relational repair.

Risk discourse often presses toward closure. Decisions must be justified. Numbers supply reasons. This is necessary in governance. It can become corrosive in personal life. When every choice demands optimisation, tenderness thins. People begin to relate as portfolios of exposure.

Return to the vigil. Its power lies in refusing optimisation. It does not ask how long is efficient. It asks who will stay. This question cuts across prediction. It grounds trust in presence rather than foresight.

The unresolved tension presses forward. As predictive tools continue to reduce uncertainty in measurable domains, will spaces for not knowing be protected—or will they be treated as inefficiencies to eliminate? The next section examines how probability itself can harden into fate. The test left hanging here is simpler. When outcomes cannot be calculated, will we still know how to wait together, or will we retreat into private risk management and call it responsibility?

Probability as the New Fate

In August 2011, in Santa Cruz, California, the police department began deploying a predictive policing tool developed by academics and later commercialised through PredPol. Officers received daily maps—small boxes on city streets—highlighting places where certain crimes were statistically more likely to occur. Patrols were adjusted. Arrests followed. The programme was framed as common sense: use data to place resources where risk was highest. Years later, as scrutiny grew, the department ended its contract, citing concerns about bias and legitimacy. The boxes had not simply predicted crime. They had reorganised policing.

Five words matter here. *The forecast became the patrol.*

This is the central move by which probability starts to behave like fate. A probability is a statement about patterns under conditions. Fate is a statement about what must be. The two are not the same. Yet public speech increasingly slides from one to the other. People say outcomes were "inevitable" because models showed high likelihood. They speak as though numbers annul alternatives. The shift is subtle. It is also morally consequential.

To theologise prediction is to treat it as more than information. It is to treat it as an authority that reveals what will happen and therefore what should be done. The language is not always religious. It appears as managerial realism, pragmatic acceptance, "following the data". Yet it carries a metaphysical flavour. The future is presented as already written, merely awaiting confirmation.

Show the behaviour. A city allocates patrols to predicted hotspots. A hospital prioritises resources based on risk scores. A lender refuses credit because a model forecasts default. Name the abstraction: inevitability. Explain the mechanism: high-probability forecasts are treated as decisive. Implication: action becomes compliance with prediction rather than deliberation about what ought to happen.

The policing example exposes the logic sharply because it involves coercive power. Predictive policing tools often draw on historical arrest and incident data. If policing has historically focused on certain neighbourhoods, the data records that focus as "crime". The model learns patterns from this record. It predicts higher risk in the same areas. Police deploy there more often. More incidents are recorded. The model's prediction appears confirmed. This is a feedback loop dressed as foresight.

Researchers Kristian Lum and William Isaac demonstrated this dynamic in 2016, showing how predictive policing based on drug arrest data reproduced racial bias because arrest data reflected enforcement practices rather than true usage patterns (*Significance*, 2016). Show the metric: arrest rates concentrate geographically. Name the abstraction: objectivity. Explain the mechanism: biased data produces biased predictions. Implication: probability becomes self-fulfilling, then mistaken for destiny.

A second named case strengthens the point. In 2016, ProPublica investigated the COMPAS risk assessment tool used in US criminal justice and reported racial disparities in false positives: Black defendants were more likely to be labelled high risk incorrectly (Angwin et al., 2016). Courts used the tool as advisory, not determinative. Yet the presence of a score shifted the moral atmosphere. A number carried weight. Judges felt pressure to justify departures. Defendants felt judged in advance.

This is where "high likelihood equals moral permission" becomes dangerous. If a system predicts someone is likely to reoffend, it becomes easier to treat them as if they already have. Preventive logic expands. A person is managed as a future threat. The abstraction "risk" becomes visible behaviour: denying parole, increasing surveillance, imposing harsher sentences. The implication is that probability authorises coercion.

It is not hard to hear the older echoes. Fate talk often produced resignation: *it was meant to be.* Providence talk sometimes produced trust: *even this is held.* Probability talk produces something stranger: a secular predestination. The future is not decreed by gods, but inferred from patterns. The effect can be the same. The possibility of change is treated as statistically negligible and therefore practically irrelevant.

The quiet motif threading this section is the threshold. A probability becomes a line. Above it, intervention. Below it, release. Thresholds simplify action. They also carry moral force. They turn continuous uncertainty into discrete categories: safe or unsafe, eligible or ineligible, trustworthy or suspicious. A person may sit barely above a threshold and yet be treated as categorically different.

A credible counter-example must be faced. Predictive tools can reduce harm when used carefully. Hotspot policing, when focused on places rather than individuals and paired with community accountability, has been associated in some studies with reduced crime without proportional increases in arrest rates. The reconciliation lies in constraints. Prediction can inform allocation. It must not become a warrant for unjust treatment. The same tool used under different norms produces different outcomes.

This returns us to language. When officials describe forecasts as inevitabilities, they obscure these norms. They present the model as neutral fate. They avoid saying, plainly, that a value choice has been made: to prioritise one kind of harm reduction over another, to accept certain errors as tolerable, to treat suspicion as manageable collateral.

Public speech reveals this drift. After disasters, commentators often cite probability and say, "We knew it would happen." After crimes, officials say, "The data showed the risk." Such phrases do not merely describe. They sanctify. They imply that responsibility lies with the future itself rather than with decisions made under uncertainty.

Spiritual traditions offered a caution here: foreknowledge does not confer permission. Even if an outcome is expected, it does not become right. A person tempted toward wrongdoing is not absolved by the predictability of temptation. A community expecting violence is not justified in acting violently pre-emptively. The moral task remains. Probability can warn. It cannot excuse.

The policing debate forces this moral clarity because the costs are borne unevenly. Communities already subject to heavy surveillance experience predictive tools as amplification, not protection. The visible behaviour is more stops, more searches, more encounters. The abstraction "safety" becomes a distributional question: safety for whom, at what cost, and with what recourse?

Some cities have begun to reckon with this. In 2020, the Los Angeles Police Commission voted to end the department's use of PredPol and similar predictive policing programmes after sustained criticism. Show the outcome: contracts terminated. Name the abstraction: legitimacy. Explain the mechanism: public trust erodes when prediction reinforces inequity. Implication: probability loses authority when its moral costs become visible.

Yet the broader drift remains. Probability language continues to expand into domains once governed by deliberation. Schools use predictive analytics to identify "at-risk" students. Employers screen candidates based on inferred retention risk. Insurers price policies based on behavioural proxies. In each case, high likelihood can become permission to treat someone as already defined by their past.

The forward tension is practical. If probability becomes the new fate, society will begin to treat statistical expectations as moral conclusions. That is a category mistake with teeth. The diagnostic question is therefore simple but demanding: when you hear a forecast described as inevitable, do you ask what assumptions produced it, and what alternatives were left untried? Probability can illuminate. Fate forecloses. The distance between them is where freedom lives.

Living Informed but Not Ruled

On 13 March 2020, in London, the UK government's Scientific Advisory Group for Emergencies (SAGE) released advice on COVID-19 that would shape national policy within days. Models projected hospital demand, deaths, and the effects of interventions. Ministers spoke with the gravitas of numbers. The public listened. Then the models shifted, as models must, when assumptions changed and new data arrived. Forecasts did not fail by changing; they failed only when people mistook them for certainty. The episode revealed a modern dilemma: we need prediction, and we over-believe it.

Five words belong here. *Models guide; they must not rule.*

Living informed but not ruled is not a call to ignore forecasts. It is a discipline of proportion. Forecasts are tools that extend perception. They allow earlier action. They reduce avoidable harm. Yet they do not absolve moral judgement. The stance proposed here holds two truths at once: prediction can be valuable, and prediction can become tyrannical when treated as fate.

The tyranny rarely arrives as coercion. It arrives as deference. Show the behaviour: refreshing a forecast repeatedly, cancelling plans because the probability line nudges upward, accepting a risk score as a verdict, deferring a difficult conversation because a compatibility metric looks low. Name the abstraction: anxiety management.

Explain the mechanism: numbers promise relief from ambiguity. Implication: the person becomes governed by probabilities rather than guided by them.

A quieter problem follows. Forecasts can shrink imagination. When likely futures are treated as the only futures, agency narrows. Plans become brittle. People begin to outsource courage. The abstraction "prudence" turns into a behaviour: never acting without numerical reassurance. The implication is paralysis disguised as wisdom.

Spiritual traditions have long insisted that wise action requires both effort and surrender. Effort means acting responsibly with the information one has. Surrender means admitting that outcomes cannot be fully controlled. This pairing is not unique to any one faith. It appears in Christian language of providence and labour, in Islamic insistence on trust in God alongside obligation, in Jewish emphasis on human responsibility under covenant, in Buddhist training to act without clinging to results. The common thread is ethical realism: choose well, then let go of what cannot be held.

Forecast culture often severs this pairing. It elevates effort as control and treats surrender as failure. Yet surrender, rightly understood, is not resignation. It is refusal to confuse probability with permission. It is commitment without omniscience.

A second named example clarifies the need for this stance. In 1986, at NASA in the United States, engineers warned of O-ring failure risk in cold weather before the Challenger launch. Management proceeded. The shuttle broke apart. The Rogers Commission later documented how organisational pressure and miscommunication distorted risk assessment. Show the behaviour: proceeding despite warnings. Name the abstraction: risk normalisation. Explain the mechanism: repeated near-misses reduce perceived danger. Implication: numbers can be ignored as easily as they can be idolised. Both are failures of judgement.

This counter-example matters because it shows the stance required is not simply scepticism about prediction. It is moral attentiveness to how prediction is used. Sometimes the problem is over-trust.

Sometimes it is selective disbelief. Both emerge when numbers are treated as political instruments rather than guides.

So what does it mean to hold plans lightly while acting responsibly? It begins by separating three questions that forecasts often collapse into one. What is likely? What is desirable? What is right? A forecast answers only the first. The other two require deliberation, community, and conscience. When a probability is allowed to answer all three, moral life is replaced by optimisation.

Visible behaviours can restore the separation. One is the deliberate pause between reading a forecast and acting on it. This pause is not sentimental. It is a small assertion of agency. Another is the habit of asking what the forecast cannot see: values, relationships, meaning, or systemic bias. The abstraction "wisdom" becomes a behaviour: interrogating assumptions rather than merely consuming outputs. The implication is humility with backbone.

The motif threading this section is the compass. A forecast is like a weather report: it tells you what conditions may be. A compass tells you where you intend to go. Many people now carry weather reports everywhere and rarely check the compass. The result is drift. Being informed becomes being steered.

Forecasts also change emotional tone. When risk is quantified, fear becomes measurable, and therefore tempting to manage obsessively. But not all fear is bad. Some fear is moral perception: awareness of what might be harmed. Spiritual traditions often treated fear of God not as terror but as reverent attentiveness. The modern analogue is a fear that keeps responsibility awake without spiralling into control.

A credible limitation must be acknowledged. For people with less power, forecasts can be protective. A flood forecast can save a family's home. A medical risk estimate can prompt early screening. A violence risk alert can trigger safeguarding. The reconciliation lies in intention and agency. Forecasts should expand options, not narrow dignity. The question is whether prediction enables preparedness or enforces compliance.

Living informed but not ruled also requires acknowledging where prediction becomes a substitute for courage. People use numbers to avoid responsibility: *the model made me do it.* They also use numbers to avoid vulnerability: *the forecast says it won't work, so I won't try.* Both are forms of surrender to prediction rather than surrender beyond it.

Spiritual teachings on surrender cut in the opposite direction. They insist that one can act without guarantees. They treat uncertainty not merely as risk but as a space where trust is practised. Trust, here, becomes a visible behaviour: choosing fidelity over reassurance, generosity over optimisation, presence over prediction.

The chapter closes with a brief reflection that does not demand confession but invites honesty. Name one domain where forecasts quietly govern you more than you admit. It may be health metrics, productivity dashboards, social approval signals, financial projections, relationship compatibility scores, or reputational risk. Identify the moment when you treat a probability as a verdict. Then ask what would change if you treated it as a guide instead—a piece of information to be weighed alongside values, commitments, and the stubborn unpredictability of life.

The unresolved tension remains. As prediction grows more sophisticated, it will become easier to justify surrendering judgement. The forward test is simple and demanding: when the next forecast arrives, will it be consulted as a compass, or obeyed as a fate?

Chapter 6
Authority After the Algorithm

At a road junction on the outskirts of Bologna in 2019, a visiting driver slowed and rolled down the window. The navigation app insisted on a sharp left turn into a narrow street. A local resident, standing beside a café, shook his head and gestured straight on. The driver hesitated, glanced at the glowing screen, and turned left. Minutes later, the car was wedged between parked vehicles, reversing awkwardly as pedestrians watched with mild amusement. The app had been wrong. The moment passed. The driver laughed. Yet the decision itself went unquestioned. When human testimony conflicted with numerical instruction, the number won.

That small scene captures a larger shift. Authority has not disappeared in the digital age; it has migrated. We still defer, still trust, still obey. What has changed is *who* or *what* receives that deference. Increasingly, it is not elders, professionals, leaders, or institutions speaking in their own voices. It is dashboards, rankings, scores, and optimisation outputs. Numbers sound cleaner. They feel calmer. They arrive without tone or temperament. They seem, somehow, more honest.

This chapter asks why. Why do algorithmic outputs carry such persuasive force, even when we know they are imperfect? Why does a quantified recommendation often feel more trustworthy than a human judgement shaped by experience and care? The answer is not simply accuracy. It is cultural. Numbers draw on long-standing stories about objectivity, impartiality, and freedom from bias. They appear to stand above interest, even when they are deeply embedded within it.

The opening movement of the chapter explores this reverence for numbers. Scores and rankings promise neutrality. They compress complexity into a single signal. They relieve us of the burden of interpretation. In contexts ranging from education to finance to navigation, people increasingly treat numerical outputs as a kind of moral shortcut. The number does not argue. It merely presents itself. Doubting it feels petulant, even irrational.

Yet numbers do not arise from nowhere. They are designed, trained, calibrated, and maintained by people within institutions. This leads to the chapter's second movement: the question of ownership and interest. Who builds these systems? Who controls the data they require? Who benefits when they are treated as authoritative? Power, in this landscape, does not always wear a uniform or speak publicly. It accumulates quietly around infrastructure, proprietary models, and technical expertise. Platform moderation decisions offer a telling case. When content is removed or amplified at scale, authority is exercised without ceremony, often without explanation, and rarely with appeal.

The chapter resists easy villains. It avoids the comfort of blaming individual engineers or executives. Instead, it traces how structural incentives shape behaviour. Platforms optimise for engagement, growth, and liability reduction. Designers work within constraints. Owners answer to markets. Authority emerges not from malice but from alignment between technical possibility and economic pressure. The result is still authority, but it is diffused, procedural, and difficult to contest.

From there, the chapter turns to leadership. Religious and civic leaders are not immune to the seductions of metrics. Some adopt algorithmic tools eagerly, seeing them as efficient aids to governance, outreach, or assessment. Others reject them wholesale, sensing a threat to judgement and pastoral care. Both responses miss something. Uncritical embrace risks surrendering moral agency to systems not designed to hold it. Total rejection risks irrelevance and nostalgia. The chapter argues for a more literate middle path: leaders who understand how systems work, where they help, and where they must be resisted or supplemented.

A concrete example grounds this argument. A community debating whether to adopt automated decision tools for resource allocation reveals the tensions clearly. Efficiency promises fairness. Automation promises consistency. Yet members worry about loss of voice, context, and mercy. The debate itself becomes a lesson in authority. Who decides how decisions are made? And on what basis?

The final movement of the chapter widens the lens. Authority is not only external. Each person carries an internal hierarchy of trust. Some voices weigh more than others. Some signals override conscience. This hierarchy is rarely examined. Metrics often slip to the top quietly, justified by convenience and cultural prestige. The chapter invites readers to notice this shift and to ask whether it aligns with their deepest commitments.

Here the book's broader themes return. Faith, in its various forms, has always involved discerning whom or what to trust. Covenants, vows, and consciences claim authority not because they are efficient, but because they bind. Metrics, by contrast, are conditional. They are useful until they are not. Treating them as ultimate authorities asks them to bear a weight they cannot sustain.

The chapter does not resolve this tension. It sharpens it. A short exercise at the end asks readers to map their own hierarchy of authorities: where numbers sit, where human judgement sits, where conscience sits, where tradition or community sits. The aim is not to dethrone metrics, but to put them back in proportion.

Authority after the algorithm is not abolished. It is redistributed. The pages that follow explore how that redistribution works, who benefits from it, and how it might be reshaped. The question left hanging is simple and unsettling. When the number and the neighbour disagree, which voice do you trust—and why?

When Numbers Sound More Honest

In June 2018, Google Maps rerouted drivers through the quiet residential streets of Leonia, New Jersey, in an attempt to avoid congestion on the George Washington Bridge. The algorithm's logic was impeccable. The outcome was not. Hundreds of cars poured through roads never designed for that volume. Residents found themselves unable to leave their driveways. The borough responded by banning non-residents during peak hours, enforced by police checkpoints. The local mayor pleaded publicly for drivers to ignore their apps. Many did not. The blue line on the screen carried more authority than the shouted warnings of neighbours standing on their own pavements.

This was not ignorance. Drivers were not unaware that an app could be wrong. It was trust. Or something adjacent to trust, cooler and harder to name. A faith that numbers, even when inconvenient, were less biased than people. A sense that calculation, stripped of tone and personality, must surely be closer to the truth.

Numbers feel clean. They arrive without hesitation. They do not hedge or apologise. When a navigation app says a journey will take forty-two minutes, the precision itself persuades. Forty-two sounds measured. It sounds earned. A local resident saying, "It'll be quicker if you go straight," sounds anecdotal, even if that resident has driven the road for twenty years. The number feels more honest.

That feeling has a history. Modern societies have spent centuries cultivating the idea that quantification disciplines judgement. From the rise of double-entry bookkeeping in Renaissance Italy to the spread of standardised testing in nineteenth-century Europe, numbers have been associated with fairness, transparency, and control. They promise to strip away favouritism and impulse. They promise equal treatment. When algorithms produce scores and rankings, they inherit this moral prestige automatically.

Consider credit scores. A three-digit number now shapes access to housing, employment, and opportunity across much of the developed world. The score does not explain itself. It does not narrate circumstances. It simply *is*. The abstraction is powerful. Behaviour is translated into a metric. The metric is treated as character. The implication follows quietly: if the number is low, something about the person must be lacking. Trust migrates from testimony to tally.

This migration is visible across domains. In education, predictive analytics flag students "at risk" based on attendance, grades, and demographic correlations. In health, risk scores estimate the likelihood of future illness, sometimes guiding who receives follow-up care. In policing, crime statistics and hotspot maps influence patrol patterns. Each system claims efficiency. Each claims objectivity. Each reduces the need for messy human judgement.

The appeal is understandable. Human testimony is partial. People lie. They forget. They favour those like themselves. Numbers seem immune to these flaws. They promise consistency. Yet this promise rests on a category error. Algorithms do not eliminate judgement. They relocate it. Decisions about what to measure, how to weight variables, and which outcomes matter are all human choices, made upstream and then hidden behind outputs.

The reverence persists because the outputs feel impersonal. A ranking does not appear to care. A score does not appear to judge. It merely reports. This is the quiet magic of quantification. Moral weight is smuggled in under the guise of measurement. The system is trusted not because it is neutral, but because it *appears* neutral.

Navigation offers a useful motif here. The map speaks with certainty. The road does not. When drivers follow an app, they outsource situational awareness to a model trained on aggregated data. The model optimises for average outcomes. The local resident optimises for context. One sees patterns. The other sees potholes. Trusting the app over the person is not irrational. It is a bet that aggregated patterns matter more than lived detail.

This bet often pays off. Most journeys guided by algorithms are faster and safer than those guided by guesswork. The counter-example matters. Algorithms genuinely outperform individuals in many narrow prediction tasks. Weather forecasts today are more accurate than folk methods of reading clouds or wind, as documented by the UK Met Office's long-term verification reports. To deny this would be perverse. Numbers deserve some of their authority.

The problem emerges when this success generalises into moral superiority. Accuracy becomes virtue. Probability becomes permission. If the model predicts congestion, drivers reroute regardless of neighbourhood impact. If the risk score predicts default, the loan is denied regardless of circumstance. If the ranking places one applicant above another, the decision feels settled. The number closes the conversation.

This closure has consequences. It alters how people speak. Terms like *inevitable*, *statistically certain*, and *data-driven* creep into everyday justification. Responsibility thins. "The system decided" replaces "I decided". The visible behaviour changes. Appeals decline. Questioning feels futile. Trust shifts from relationship to representation.

Cultural stories sustain this shift. Enlightenment ideals framed reason as the enemy of superstition. Measurement became a tool of liberation. To quantify was to free oneself from arbitrary power. Algorithms inherit this emancipatory narrative, even when deployed by powerful institutions. A platform's ranking algorithm is experienced not as authority imposed, but as reality revealed.

Yet cracks appear. In 2016, ProPublica analysed the COMPAS risk assessment tool used in US courts and found racial disparities in false positives and negatives. The score's authority masked embedded assumptions about data and policing practices. Judges trusted the number. Defendants struggled to contest it. The counter-example does not invalidate risk assessment entirely. It reveals a limit. Numbers can reproduce injustice while sounding impartial.

Reconciling these facts requires care. The aim is not to romanticise human judgement or demonise metrics. Humans are biased. Numbers can help correct that. The aim is to see clearly where authority is being exercised and on what grounds. A navigation app optimises travel time. It does not optimise civic harmony. A credit score predicts repayment. It does not measure worth. When numbers speak outside their domain, they still sound confident.

This is why they persuade. Confidence is contagious. Precision seduces. A journey time displayed to the minute feels more actionable than a neighbour's shrug. A score out of 850 feels more solid than a conversation about circumstances. The motif returns: the clean line on the map, glowing and certain, versus the human voice, fallible and embodied.

The implication is not withdrawal but discernment. To trust numbers appropriately requires knowing what they were built to do and what they were never meant to answer. That knowledge is unevenly distributed. Time-conscious professionals rely on metrics because metrics save time. Students accept rankings because rankings simplify choice. Systems are trusted because they reduce friction.

The unresolved tension lies here. If numbers continue to sound more honest than people, even when they are not more just, what happens to testimony, responsibility, and dissent? When the app and the resident disagree, the choice feels trivial. Scaled up, it is not. The chapter leaves the reader with a forward test: the next time a number contradicts a human voice, pause. Ask what the number knows. Ask what it cannot know. Then decide who deserves your trust.

Designers, Owners, and Interests

On 6 January 2021, as violence unfolded at the US Capitol in Washington, D.C., Twitter began attaching labels to misleading claims about the election and later suspended thousands of accounts linked to coordinated activity. Facebook removed content and groups, while YouTube took down videos that violated its policies. Within days, the platforms made a decision that would become a defining symbol of private authority: on 8 January 2021, Twitter permanently suspended President Donald Trump's account. The outcome was immediate. A head of state lost direct access to a global audience through a privately owned system.

Five words belong here. *A company drew the line.*

That line is not drawn by "the algorithm" alone. It is drawn by designers, owners, policy teams, and incentives that shape what algorithms are trained to do. When people say, "the platform decided," they often picture an automated, neutral process. In reality, moderation at scale is a hybrid of code and governance. It is one of the clearest places to see how power concentrates around data, infrastructure, and expertise—and how authority is exercised without the familiar rituals of public accountability.

Begin with the designers. Engineers and data scientists build ranking and detection systems to meet objectives: reduce harmful content, retain users, comply with law, protect advertisers, manage public perception. These objectives can conflict. A system optimised for engagement will often reward emotionally charged content. A system optimised for safety may suppress legitimate speech. Designers do not choose these trade-offs alone. They implement them. Yet implementation is itself a moral act. Decisions about what counts as "harm," which signals trigger enforcement, and how errors are tolerated become embedded in code.

Show the behaviour: a video is removed. An account is shadow-banned. A warning label is attached. Name the abstraction: "community standards." Explain the mechanism: policies translated into rules and machine-learning classifiers. Implication: governance becomes procedural, enforced by systems rather than deliberation in public.

The owners matter as much as the designers. Platforms are not merely communication utilities; they are businesses with fiduciary duties and market pressures. Their revenues often depend on advertising, which depends on attention, which depends on content that keeps people engaged. This is structural incentive, not personal villainy. Even well-intentioned executives operate within a logic where growth and risk reduction are rewarded. When a platform moderates, it does so in a field of constraints: legal liability, reputational threat, advertiser pressure, user backlash, and competitive dynamics.

This is why authority concentrates. Data is not evenly distributed. The largest platforms possess the richest behavioural datasets, the most extensive infrastructure, and the deepest pools of technical expertise. These assets reinforce each other. More users generate more data. More data improves models. Better models improve user experience. The cycle tightens. Smaller competitors struggle to replicate it. Power becomes infrastructural.

A second named example illustrates the stakes. In 2016, the European Commission opened an antitrust case against Google regarding the prominence of its own comparison-shopping service in search results. In 2017, the Commission fined Google €2.42 billion and ordered changes. The case was not about speech but about ranking. Yet ranking is authority. It determines what is seen first. Show the behaviour: preferential placement in results. Name the abstraction: fairness. Explain the mechanism: platform control over distribution. Implication: economic and informational power converge in the same interface.

Moderation decisions are a special kind of ranking: the decision to remove is the decision to make something unfindable. That is a form of power stronger than recommendation. It is often justified. It is sometimes contested. What matters is who gets to do it, under what standards, and with what appeals.

The platform moderation case demonstrates authority exercised at scale. Traditional public authority is bounded by geography and subject to explicit constitutional or legal frameworks. Platform authority is global by default and governed by terms-of-service agreements few read. The abstraction "legitimacy" becomes visible behaviour when users accept decisions they cannot contest. The implication is a new kind of sovereignty: private, procedural, and pervasive.

It is tempting to demonise individual decision-makers. This temptation should be resisted. Many people working in trust and safety teams are acutely aware of the harms they are trying to limit—harassment, incitement, exploitation, misinformation. Their work is difficult and often traumatising. The point is not to paint them as censors. The point is to notice how institutional incentives and technical constraints shape outcomes beyond any one person's intent.

Here a credible limitation complicates the critique. At scale, some automation is necessary. No human team can manually review every post, video, and comment generated by billions of users. Machine learning helps detect spam, violent content, and coordinated manipulation quickly. It reduces harm. It is, in many cases, a form of care. The reconciliation lies in acknowledging necessity without granting infallibility. Automation can support governance; it cannot replace legitimacy.

Legitimacy requires explanation, consistency, and recourse. Yet these are precisely what large-scale systems struggle to provide. Machine classifiers generate false positives and false negatives. Policies evolve under pressure. Enforcement varies across languages and regions. Users experience moderation as arbitrary. The abstraction "trust" becomes a behaviour: migrating to alternative platforms or self-censoring. The implication is social fragmentation.

The concentration of expertise deepens the asymmetry. Platforms can hire specialists, commission research, and build internal measurement systems to monitor content trends. Ordinary users cannot. Even governments struggle. When a platform claims that a moderation change reduced harmful content by a certain percentage, the public often cannot verify it. Numbers sound more honest, even here. Authority is reinforced by metrics that only the platform can produce.

The motif threading this section is the gate. Platforms are gates to public speech and commerce. Gatekeeping is not new; editors, broadcasters, and publishers have always shaped distribution. The difference is scale and opacity. A newspaper editor can be named. A platform's ranking logic cannot. The gate is staffed by code.

This produces a shift in how power is contested. In older frameworks, citizens petitioned elected officials or challenged laws in court. In platform governance, people appeal through forms and automated messages. Policy debates become customer service interactions. The abstraction "rights" becomes "violations." The implication is profound: moral and political questions are reframed as compliance issues.

Return to January 2021. The decision to suspend a head of state revealed how private authority can intersect with public life. Some applauded. Some protested. Almost everyone recognised the strangeness. It was not simply about the individual. It was about who had the power to silence—and what procedures made that power legitimate.

The forward tension remains unresolved. Platforms will continue to exercise authority at scale because they mediate attention. Designers will continue to encode values into systems because systems require objectives. Owners will continue to respond to incentives because businesses do. The diagnostic question, then, is not whether platforms will govern. They already do. The question is whether their governance will remain a private gate, controlled by internal interests and opaque metrics—or whether societies will demand forms of accountability commensurate with the authority these systems now wield.

Leaders in the Age of Metrics

In March 2019, the city council of Amsterdam voted to suspend the use of a predictive analytics system known as SyRI, designed to identify welfare fraud by combining data from multiple public agencies. The decision followed months of debate involving municipal officials, legal scholars, community advocates, and faith leaders concerned about transparency and discrimination. The system promised efficiency. It also promised certainty. What it could not offer was explanation. In February 2020, a Dutch court ruled that SyRI violated human rights, citing the opacity of its risk models. A local tool became a public reckoning.

The meeting that preceded the suspension was unremarkable in form. People gathered around tables. Arguments were exchanged. What made it notable was the question beneath the procedural surface: should leaders defer to a system that claims superior judgement, or should they slow it down, interrogate it, and risk being accused of standing in the way of progress?

Leadership has always involved mediating between knowledge and judgement. Metrics sharpen that tension. When an algorithm presents a ranked list, a score, or a forecast, it arrives with an implicit demand: *trust me*. Some leaders comply readily. Others recoil. The first group treats data-driven tools as neutral advisers. The second treats them as threats to moral agency. Both responses miss something essential.

Consider religious leadership. Many congregations now use analytics to track attendance patterns, giving patterns of giving, and engagement across programmes. Software dashboards display trends that once emerged only through long familiarity. The behaviour is clear: decisions about staffing, outreach, and scheduling increasingly reference metrics. Name the abstraction: stewardship. Explain the mechanism: quantification promises better allocation of limited resources. Implication: pastoral judgement risks being narrowed to what can be measured.

The opposite reaction also appears. Some leaders reject metrics entirely, insisting that spiritual life cannot be quantified without being corrupted. They avoid digital tools and frame resistance as fidelity. This posture protects against reductionism. It can also slide into romanticism. Communities still make decisions. Without evidence, those decisions rely on intuition and hierarchy. The risk is not purity, but blindness.

Civic leadership displays the same polarity. Mayors adopt "smart city" dashboards to monitor traffic, crime, and energy use in real time. Councillors praise responsiveness. Critics warn of surveillance and bias. In some cases, leaders defer excessively, allowing metrics to dictate policy without deliberation. In others, they ban tools outright, forfeiting potential benefits. Neither extreme cultivates wisdom.

A grounded example illustrates the middle path. In 2018, the city of Toronto debated its participation in Sidewalk Labs' proposed Quayside development, a data-rich urban project backed by Alphabet. The proposal promised efficient services and evidence-based planning. It also raised concerns about data ownership and democratic control. Civic leaders did not simply accept or reject the project. They convened consultations, commissioned independent reviews, and ultimately imposed conditions. The project was later abandoned, but the process mattered. Leaders neither surrendered authority nor clung to ignorance. They demanded literacy.

Literacy is the quiet motif here. Not fluency in code, but competence in interpretation. Leaders do not need to build models. They need to ask what models assume, what they optimise, and where they fail. This requires a shift in posture. Metrics become inputs, not verdicts. The visible behaviour changes: meetings include questions about data provenance, error rates, and impacts on marginal groups. The abstraction "responsibility" becomes concrete.

A credible counter-example tempers this argument. In emergency contexts, leaders may need to act quickly on imperfect data. During public health crises, dashboards tracking hospital capacity and infection rates inform urgent decisions. Delay costs lives. Here, deference to metrics can be appropriate. Reconciliation lies in context. Speed does not absolve leaders of later review. Temporary reliance should not harden into permanent abdication.

The tension is particularly sharp for leaders formed in traditions that emphasise discernment. Discernment is not instinct. It is cultivated judgement, tested in community, attentive to consequences. Algorithms compress time. They promise answers without waiting. Leaders face pressure to match that pace. Constituents expect efficiency. Funders expect outcomes. Platforms reward responsiveness. Slowness looks like weakness.

Yet slowness has a function. It creates space to notice who benefits and who bears cost. When a council debates an automated housing allocation system, metrics can show throughput and reduced processing time. They rarely show the experience of applicants flagged as low priority. Leaders who insist on hearing those stories are not anti-data. They are completing the picture.

Pair abstraction with behaviour again. "Efficiency" appears as shorter queues. "Fairness" appears as appeal mechanisms that work. "Trust" appears as public acceptance of decisions even when outcomes disappoint. Metrics can support these goods. They cannot define them.

Religious leaders face an additional layer. Algorithmic authority competes with moral authority. When congregants trust health apps more than communal counsel, or social media feeds more than teaching, leaders may feel displaced. Some respond by borrowing the language of metrics, citing growth statistics or engagement rates to validate ministry. Others double down on charisma. Neither response addresses the underlying shift in trust.

The literate middle path acknowledges that authority now circulates through systems. Leaders cannot pretend otherwise. They can, however, model how to relate to that authority without being ruled by it. This involves public reasoning. When a leader explains why they overrode a recommendation, they make judgement visible. When they follow a recommendation, they explain why it aligns with values. Silence cedes ground.

The SyRI case returns as a touchstone. Dutch leaders did not claim the system was evil. They asked whether it met standards of transparency and proportionality. The court's ruling provided a framework. Leaders accepted constraint. Authority was redistributed.

The unresolved tension remains. As metrics proliferate, leaders will increasingly be judged by numbers they do not control. Performance indicators shape careers. Congregational dashboards shape reputations. The forward test is simple to state and hard to practice: when the metric and your judgement diverge, which do you follow—and how do you explain that choice to those who trust you?

Rewriting Our Hierarchy of Trust

In September 2008, in New York City, Lehman Brothers filed for bankruptcy after months in which major institutions had relied on risk models and credit ratings that treated complex mortgage products as manageable. The models did not invent greed, nor did they force anyone's hand. They did something subtler. They supplied reassurance. Ratings stamped with AAA signalled safety. Value-at-Risk metrics suggested losses were containable. When the assumptions cracked, the numbers did not merely fail; they were revealed as insufficient grounds for trust. The outcome was not just financial collapse. It was a crisis of authority.

Five words matter here. *The metrics promised too much.*

This chapter has traced how authority migrates toward numbers, not because numbers are always right, but because they feel impartial, scalable, and calm. The final task is not to unmask metrics as fraudulent. It is to re-order them. Metrics are tools. They are not covenant partners. They can inform. They cannot bind.

A hierarchy of trust is the set of authorities that a person, or a community, instinctively consults when choices become costly. Some authorities speak loudly—laws, employers, institutions, family expectations. Others whisper—conscience, prayer, vows, the remembered counsel of a friend. In a metric-saturated culture, numbers tend to climb this hierarchy quietly. They arrive embedded in interfaces, wrapped in defaults, presented as neutrality. Over time, they begin to feel like the final word.

Show the behaviour. A person changes a decision because a compatibility score is low. A manager rejects an applicant because an automated ranking places them below a threshold. A driver ignores the neighbour's warning because the navigation app shows a faster route. Name the abstraction: trust. Explain the mechanism: numerical outputs present themselves as objective adjudicators. Implication: judgement is transferred from relationships to representations.

This transfer matters because metrics are conditional by nature. They depend on data quality, modelling assumptions, and objectives chosen by designers. A credit score predicts repayment under certain economic conditions; it does not measure honesty. A health risk score estimates likelihood of an outcome given populations; it does not define a person's future. A content ranking reflects engagement incentives; it does not track truth. Metrics have domains. When they are asked to rule outside those domains, they become counterfeit authorities.

The motif threading this section is the altar. An altar is where ultimate trust is placed, where one offers something costly—time, loyalty, sacrifice. Modern life has many altars. Some are visible: money, reputation, control. Metrics can become altars when they are treated as unquestionable and when people offer their agency to them without noticing.

This is not merely an individual problem. Institutions develop hierarchies of trust too. When leaders rely on dashboards more than testimonies, they communicate what counts as real. When governments cite models to justify decisions without explaining values, they shift accountability from deliberation to prediction. When platforms display rankings as though they were natural order, they present design as destiny. In each case, the hierarchy of trust is rewritten publicly.

The alternative is not to return to pure intuition. Human judgement is fallible and biased. We have already seen how metrics can correct arbitrary power. The credible limitation of a purely "conscience-first" approach is that conscience can be malformed. It can rationalise harm. It can confuse preference with principle. The reconciliation lies in layered authority. Metrics can interrogate intuition. Conscience can interrogate metrics. Community can interrogate both.

Faith traditions offer language for this layering without forcing doctrinal agreement. Conscience, in many traditions, is not the voice of private desire but the capacity to perceive moral obligation. Covenant is not merely a contract; it is a binding promise that persists through inconvenience. Prayer is not a technique for prediction; it is a practice of alignment. These are deeper authorities than metrics because they speak to what ought to be done, not merely to what is likely.

Metrics, by contrast, excel at certain questions: how often, how many, how quickly, how likely. They are weak at questions of meaning: why, for whom, at what cost, and what is worth preserving. When metrics rise to the top of the hierarchy, the questions at the bottom begin to sound irrelevant. That is how moral drift occurs—quietly, through the narrowing of what counts as evidence.

A second named example clarifies this narrowing. In 1986, the Challenger disaster revealed how engineers' concerns were overridden in part by managerial interpretations of risk. The problem was not absence of data, but a hierarchy that privileged schedule and perceived acceptability over embodied warning. Show the behaviour: proceeding despite dissent. Name the abstraction: institutional trust. Explain the mechanism: certain metrics and pressures outrank testimony. Implication: disaster can follow from misplaced authority as easily as from ignorance.

So how does one rewrite a hierarchy of trust without performing purity or nostalgia? It begins by noticing where authority is already operating. Most people do not consciously choose to trust metrics; they are trained into it. A number appears. It looks precise. It shortens decision time. The convenience is real. Yet convenience is not a moral argument.

The short exercise that closes the chapter is designed to make this hierarchy visible, not to prescribe a single right order. Choose one recent decision—small is fine—where you felt uncertain. Identify which authorities you consulted. Perhaps it was a score, a forecast, a friend's counsel, a gut feeling, a professional guideline, a religious teaching, or a memory of an earlier mistake. Then ask, without theatre, which of these authorities was decisive. Which voice ended the conversation?

Now ask a harder question. If that decisive authority had been wrong, where would responsibility have landed? Would you have said, "I chose," or "the system said"? This is not a linguistic quibble. It reveals whether you have retained authorship or delegated it.

A further question sharpens the contrast between metric and covenant. What authority would you obey even when it costs you? Metrics are abandoned when they inconvenience. Covenants are kept precisely when they inconvenience. If the highest authority in your life changes whenever the optimisation target changes, it is not an authority. It is a preference dressed as necessity.

The chapter does not demand that everyone place religious commitments above metrics. It does not resolve theology. It does insist that ultimate trust cannot safely be given to systems designed for conditional prediction. Even secular conscience requires commitments that cannot be reduced to data. Human dignity, fairness, mercy, truthfulness—these are not merely outcomes to optimise; they are principles that sometimes require accepting inefficiency.

The unresolved tension remains vivid because the world will not become less quantified. Metrics will become more persuasive, more embedded, more personalised. The forward test is therefore ongoing. When the next number appears, glowing with confidence, will you treat it as a tool within its domain, or as an oracle? And when your conscience, your community, or your covenant speaks against the number, will you know how to hear it—and how to act?

Chapter 7
Communities on the Digital Plains

On Easter Sunday in April 2020, as lockdowns silenced church bells across Europe and North America, millions of people gathered for worship without leaving their kitchens. Livestreams replaced pews. Comment threads replaced whispered greetings. In Rome, Pope Francis presided over a near-empty St Peter's Basilica while viewers from São Paulo to Seoul watched on phones and laptops. The ritual endured. The assembly changed. Belief remained recognisable, yet the shape of belonging had shifted in ways that were not easily reversible.

Communities have always been spatial. They have gathered bodies as well as convictions. They have relied on proximity, shared rhythms, and the slow accumulation of trust. Digital platforms disrupt each of these conditions at once. They collapse distance, accelerate interaction, and reward visibility over fidelity. The result is not the disappearance of community, but its reconfiguration. Faith migrates onto the plains of the feed—vast, open, exposed to weather patterns it does not control.

This chapter begins from a simple claim with complex consequences: belief is never merely private. It is formed, tested, and sustained in company. Stories are told together. Symbols are shared. Authority emerges through recognition. When those processes move onto platforms designed for scale and engagement, community life inherits the logic of those systems whether it intends to or not.

The first movement of the chapter considers belief and belonging under algorithmic mediation. Digital access has lowered barriers that once excluded the isolated, the ill, and the geographically distant. Livestreamed rituals allow participation where none was possible before. Online prayer groups convene across time zones, sharing intentions in real time. The gift is genuine. Yet something thins. Local bonds, once reinforced by regular, embodied presence, compete with global affinity. A person may feel deeply connected to a dispersed group while remaining unknown to the neighbour next door. Belonging expands. It also floats.

The second movement turns to authority and attention. Algorithms do not merely distribute content; they rank voices. In spiritual spaces, this has given rise to charismatic influencers whose reach dwarfs that of traditional leaders. Sermons become clips. Devotion becomes branded. Attention begins to stand in for discernment. When a message goes viral, it acquires the sheen of validation. The chapter does not dismiss this outright. Many voices amplified online are thoughtful, generous, and rigorous. The question is structural: what happens to authority when it is measured by views rather than trust, by shares rather than service?

Conflict sharpens these dynamics. Platforms reward strong emotion and rapid response. Outrage travels faster than nuance. Within digital faith communities, disagreements that once unfolded slowly now flare publicly. Ancient warnings about gossip and division find new relevance when comment threads spiral. Yet alternatives exist. Moderated forums with clear norms demonstrate that disagreement need not be performative. Slower exchanges allow listening. The chapter explores how practices of restraint can resist platform incentives without retreating from public engagement.

The closing movement looks forward. Digital spaces are not neutral containers, but neither are they destiny. Communities can inhabit them differently. Experiments in smaller, invitation-based gatherings show how attention can be redirected from performance to presence. Hybrid practices—combining online connection with in-person commitment—suggest a way to remain accessible without becoming diffuse. Rituals that privilege listening over broadcasting offer a counter-rhythm to the feed.

Throughout, a recurring image frames the discussion: the plain. Plains are open and fertile, but exposed. They invite movement and exchange. They also lack shelter. Communities on the digital plains must learn how to pitch tents—structures of care, authority, and patience—without imagining they can rebuild the village unchanged. The chapter does not offer a blueprint. It offers questions sharpened by observation. What kind of belonging do platforms cultivate by default? Which voices rise, and why? How might communities reclaim practices that sustain depth amid reach?

The chapter ends without resolution, but not without direction. It invites readers to notice where their own sense of belonging is being shaped—by gatherings they attend, feeds they scroll, and voices they trust. The plains are wide. The weather is unpredictable. Communities will form there regardless. The task is not to flee the landscape, but to learn how to dwell within it with intention, humility, and care.

Belief, Belonging, and the Feed

In April 2020, during the first months of the COVID-19 lockdown in the United Kingdom, the Church of England reported that its online services were being watched more than 5.4 million times each week, compared with average pre-pandemic in-person attendance of under one million. On a Tuesday evening in Birmingham, a WhatsApp prayer group linked to a small parish added twelve new members in a single day, including participants joining from Kenya and Canada. The church building was closed. The community was not.

Five words carry the change. *The gathering moved screenside.*

Belief has never been solitary. Even the hermit withdraws into a story shared with others. Faith traditions form people through repetition, witness, and mutual recognition. Creeds are spoken aloud. Songs are sung together. Stories are handed on until they shape instinct. Belonging precedes belief as often as it follows it. One learns what to trust by watching whom others trust.

Digital platforms do not erase this social dimension. They intensify it while altering its texture. When belief enters the feed, it becomes visible, portable, and continuously present. Livestreamed rituals allow worship to travel. Prayer requests circulate instantly. Scripture verses appear between advertisements and headlines. The behaviour is concrete: a phone vibrates with a notification inviting participation. Name the abstraction: community. Explain the mechanism: platforms collapse distance and time, making gathering possible without co-presence. Implication: access expands, while the meaning of "together" shifts.

The gift is undeniable. People who are homebound, geographically isolated, or marginalised by traditional structures find entry points once denied to them. Online prayer groups exemplify this change. A participant types an intention. Others respond with words, emojis, or silent attention. The exchange is real. Comfort is felt. For many, this is not a substitute but a lifeline. Studies of digital religion, such as Heidi Campbell's work on online faith communities (2013), document how these spaces generate genuine solidarity and sustained participation.

Yet the feed is not a neutral commons. It is governed by ranking systems designed to maximise engagement. Belief content competes with everything else for attention. This competition subtly reshapes expression. Prayers become shorter. Messages become more declarative. Symbols condense into images. Theology migrates into memes.

Meme theology is not trivial by default. Aphorisms have always carried belief. Icons and parables compress meaning. The difference lies in circulation speed and context collapse. A meme travels detached from its originating community. It invites affirmation without accountability. The visible behaviour is a "share" without conversation. Name the abstraction: witness. Explain the mechanism: platforms reward content that elicits quick reaction. Implication: belief risks flattening into slogans that gather approval rather than cultivate understanding.

Local bonds feel the pressure. When belonging is mediated primarily through feeds, presence becomes optional. One can attend multiple communities without being claimed by any. The parish down the road competes with a global network curated by algorithms. The trade-off appears efficient. Time is saved. Choice expands. Yet commitment thins. Sociologist Robert Putnam's earlier diagnosis of declining civic participation finds a new expression here: connection without obligation.

A counter-example complicates the picture. In some cases, online belonging strengthens local ties rather than eroding them. Hybrid communities use digital tools to coordinate care, share information, and sustain contact between physical gatherings. During lockdowns, many congregations reported increased pastoral contact through messaging platforms, even as buildings closed. The reconciliation lies in intention. Platforms amplify tendencies already present. They can disperse attention or focus it.

The motif threading this section is the table. Traditionally, tables gather people into shared time. Digital feeds resemble endless tables where everyone speaks at once. Food is abundant. Conversation fragments. One can leave without being noticed. Belonging becomes ambient.

Trust shifts accordingly. In embodied communities, trust is built through repeated interaction and mutual vulnerability. In feeds, trust often follows familiarity and frequency. The voice encountered most often feels authoritative. The behaviour is measurable: algorithms surface content similar to what has already engaged the user. Name the abstraction: authority. Explain the mechanism: repetition creates perceived reliability. Implication: belonging begins to form around visibility rather than responsibility.

Online prayer groups illustrate both promise and peril. Members may share intimate concerns with people they have never met. This can be profoundly supportive. It can also bypass safeguards present in local communities. Who holds confidentiality? Who notices absence? Who intervenes when harm appears? These questions are not theoretical. They surface when groups grow beyond manageable scale or when conflict arises.

The feed encourages breadth. Faith communities have historically relied on depth. Breadth brings diversity and reach. Depth requires patience and friction. The two are not enemies, but they do pull in different directions. Platforms incline toward the former. Communities must work deliberately to preserve the latter.

No nostalgia is required to see the difference. Ancient gatherings were not idyllic. They excluded as often as they embraced. Digital access corrects some of those failures. The limitation of romanticising locality must be acknowledged. Yet it remains true that belonging thickens where people are known beyond what they post.

The unresolved tension at the close of this section is practical rather than theoretical. As belief continues to flow through feeds, communities must decide what kind of belonging they will cultivate. Will participation be counted by views or by presence? Will symbols invite contemplation or reaction? Will access lead to care, or to dispersion?

The forward test is simple to pose. The next time you encounter a prayer, ritual, or teaching in your feed, ask not only whether you agree, but where it is trying to gather you. Toward a people who will notice if you are missing, or toward an endless table where belonging is felt, briefly, and then replaced by the next scroll.

Influencers, Attention, and Authority

In March 2018, in Dallas, Texas, a preacher named Michael Todd delivered a sermon at Transformation Church that included an extended visual illustration: he spat into his hand and rubbed it on a congregant's face to dramatise a gospel story about healing. A clip of the moment circulated online within days. Outrage followed. Defences followed. Millions watched. The church issued explanations. Commentators debated reverence, spectacle, and context. Few viewers had been in the room. Yet the clip shaped perceptions of the preacher and the message far beyond the congregation that had gathered that day.

Five words belong here. *The sermon became a clip.*

That transition matters because platforms do not amplify sermons; they amplify *what can travel.* The logic of attention selects for moments that are vivid, compressible, and emotionally legible at speed. Within spiritual spaces, this logic has accelerated the rise of influencers: individuals whose authority is increasingly measured by visibility—views, shares, followers—rather than by the older markers of formation, accountability, and service.

Show the behaviour. A charismatic speaker posts short devotional videos, and the algorithm surfaces them repeatedly. Name the abstraction: authority. Explain the mechanism: frequent exposure creates familiarity, and familiarity is read as trustworthiness. Implication: attention becomes a proxy for spiritual weight.

This proxy is not entirely new. Religious movements have always had charismatic figures, travelling preachers, and widely copied texts. The printing press multiplied reach. Radio and television extended it. What is new is the speed of amplification and the intimacy of delivery. A sermon in a feed arrives inches from the face, in private, late at night, without community mediation. The voice feels personal. It feels chosen. The platform presents it as *for you.*

Algorithms intensify this by rewarding content that keeps people watching. Platforms measure retention: how long viewers stay before scrolling. They measure interaction: comments, likes, shares. Content that triggers these signals is promoted. In spiritual contexts, this selects for particular forms: the inspiring testimony, the sharp rebuke, the tearful confession, the confident prophecy, the quick moral verdict. Nuance struggles. Silence disappears. The abstraction "edification" becomes a metric: engagement rate.

Branded devotion emerges naturally in this environment. Influencers often package spiritual practice with a recognisable aesthetic: typography, colour palettes, music beds, catchphrases, merch. Branding is not inherently cynical. It can help people find content and build community. Yet it also reshapes the relation between message and messenger. The messenger becomes a product. The follower becomes an audience. The covenantal bonds of community are replaced by the looser ties of fandom.

A second named example makes the dynamic concrete. In February 2023, the "He Gets Us" advertising campaign aired a Super Bowl advert presenting Jesus as a figure of radical empathy. The campaign's online presence included highly shareable graphics and short clips designed for social distribution. Show the behaviour: people share religious messaging as advertising content. Name the abstraction: evangelism. Explain the mechanism: message designed for virality and broad appeal. Implication: spiritual communication adopts marketing logics, with attention as the key currency.

The shift is not simply stylistic. It changes accountability. Traditional religious authority is usually embedded in institutions and communities: churches, mosques, synagogues, temples, orders, councils. Leaders are answerable to peers and to local realities. When an influencer speaks online, their audience may be global and unstructured. Criticism becomes comment-thread combat. Correction becomes content. Sometimes there is no correction at all. Authority floats.

This floating authority is particularly potent because the platform's recommendation systems can mimic discernment. Users experience a sense of being guided: *this is the message you needed.* The behaviour is visible: one watches a clip, then another, then another, each more aligned with the viewer's mood. Name the abstraction: guidance. Explain the mechanism: algorithms infer preference and serve matching content. Implication: spiritual direction is simulated through pattern matching rather than relationship.

Here a credible counter-example must be acknowledged. Digital platforms have amplified voices that institutions ignored or marginalised. Survivors of abuse have found language and solidarity online. Theologians from minority traditions have reached audiences previously inaccessible. Pastors in small towns have offered careful teaching that travels widely. The reconciliation lies in distinguishing amplification from authority. Reach can be a gift without being a credential.

The motif threading this section is the pulpit. The pulpit once stood in a particular place, before a particular people, within a shared rhythm of worship and life. The digital pulpit is everywhere, always on, and measured constantly. The preacher now speaks under the gaze of metrics. Views and shares arrive as immediate feedback. This feedback shapes what is said, even unconsciously. The abstraction "faithfulness" becomes difficult to separate from "performance".

When attention becomes the proxy for authority, several distortions follow. First, urgency crowds out patience. Influencers are rewarded for frequent posting. Many spiritual practices, however, require slowness. Reflection does not trend. Second, certainty crowds out humility. Content that claims decisive answers often performs better than content that admits complexity. Third, conflict crowds out care. Public disagreement generates engagement, and engagement generates distribution.

The Michael Todd clip illustrates the mechanics. A single moment, removed from context, becomes a moral spectacle. People judge without proximity. Defenders excuse without scrutiny. The platform thrives on polarisation. Meanwhile, the local pastoral questions—what happened in the room, what harm was done, what accountability is appropriate—are drowned out by the roar of attention. Authority is redistributed, but not necessarily improved.

There is also a quieter harm. When followers treat a digital voice as primary spiritual authority, they may neglect local communities that could hold them in love and challenge. The behaviour is subtle: attending online devotionals while skipping embodied gathering, relying on influencers for counsel rather than trusted mentors. Name the abstraction: belonging. Explain the mechanism: parasocial intimacy feels like relationship. Implication: the believer becomes an audience member rather than a participant.

Parasocial intimacy is not merely a media term; it is a spiritual phenomenon. A person can feel seen by someone who does not know they exist. This can comfort. It can also mislead. A pastor who sits at a bedside cannot be replaced by an influencer who posts a comforting quote. The difference is mutuality. Mutuality binds. Attention does not.

The middle path is not to scorn influencers or to romanticise pre-digital authority. Traditional institutions have failed grievously in many contexts. Digital spaces have brought necessary critique. The more literate path is to ask what forms of authority are being cultivated by the platform's incentives and how communities can counterbalance them.

Counterbalancing begins with visibility about metrics. When leaders acknowledge that platforms reward certain kinds of content, they help communities resist confusion. It also involves intentional accountability structures: advisory boards, peer review, transparent correction processes. These measures are not performative; they are forms of moral architecture.

For viewers, the discipline is discernment. Not the vague notion of "being discerning", but a concrete behaviour: tracing authority to accountability. Who can challenge this voice? Who knows this person offline? Who bears the cost of their mistakes? These questions are ancient. They become urgent when the feed becomes a primary catechist.

The unresolved tension remains. Digital platforms will continue to elevate voices that capture attention. Some will be wise. Some will be reckless. Many will be somewhere in between. The forward test is personal and communal: when a spiritual message reaches you through the feed and feels compelling, will you treat its popularity as proof of its authority—or will you ask what the platform has trained you to mistake for truth?

Conflict, Outrage, and Division

On 4 October 2017, in Menlo Park, California, Facebook changed its reaction buttons by adding new options—"love", "wow", "haha", "sad", and "angry"—and began incorporating these reactions more deeply into how its News Feed ranked content. The "angry" reaction was not introduced as a weapon. It was introduced as a way to express feeling. Yet it became a measurable signal. Posts that provoked strong emotion could rise in visibility. In the years that followed, internal research and external reporting repeatedly noted what users already sensed: outrage travels well when a platform rewards it.

Five words belong here. *Anger became a ranking signal.*

Digital faith communities have not invented conflict. Religious history is crowded with schisms, heresies, councils, reforms, and revivals. Disagreement is often unavoidable when ultimate claims are involved. Yet platforms alter the conditions under which disagreement unfolds. They compress time, flatten context, and publish every argument to the crowd. They reward heat over light. When conflict enters the feed, it does not simply occur; it performs.

Show the behaviour. A doctrinal dispute erupts under a viral sermon clip. Comments pile up within minutes. Screenshots travel to rival groups. Name the abstraction: "accountability". Explain the mechanism: public criticism is rewarded by visibility and social reinforcement. Implication: correction becomes spectacle, and spectacle hardens positions.

Ancient traditions anticipated this dynamic in a different vocabulary. Warnings against gossip, slander, and divisive speech appear across scriptures and monastic rules. The moral concern is not merely politeness. It is spiritual formation. Words shape souls. Communities can be destroyed by the pleasure of condemnation. The platform does not need to invent this pleasure. It only needs to quantify and reward it.

A useful empirical anchor comes from outside religious studies. In 2018, researchers at MIT published a study in *Science* showing that false news spread faster and farther on Twitter than true news, in part because novelty and emotional response drive sharing (Vosoughi, Roy, and Aral, 2018). The claim is not that faith communities are uniquely prone to falsehood. The implication is structural: platforms amplify content that triggers quick reaction. Outrage is efficient. Care is slow.

This efficiency shifts how people argue. In a face-to-face community, disagreement is tempered by social cost. One must see the other person next week. One must live alongside them. Online, the cost is often lower and the audience larger. The behaviour is visible: harsher language, quicker accusations, more absolutist framing. Name the abstraction: courage. Explain the mechanism: performing righteousness for an audience feels like bravery. Implication: humility is displaced by signalling.

Polarisation is not only about ideas. It is about belonging. In digital spaces, identity forms quickly around positions. People join groups that affirm them, then absorb the group's emotional tone. Outrage becomes a bonding agent. To be furious together is to be united. The abstraction "unity" becomes a behaviour: coordinated pile-ons against outsiders. The implication is tragic: community coherence is purchased through contempt.

Yet this is not inevitable. The counter-example matters precisely because it shows that platform logic can be resisted. Consider a moderated forum such as r/AskHistorians on Reddit, which is known for strict rules, active moderation, and a culture that privileges evidence over reaction. The subject matter is not faith, but the structure is instructive. Comments are removed if they do not meet standards. Contributors cite sources. Arguments unfold with restraint. Show the behaviour: slow, curated discussion. Name the abstraction: trust. Explain the mechanism: norms and enforcement change incentives. Implication: disagreement becomes inquiry rather than warfare.

Faith communities can adopt similar architectures, even within mainstream platforms. Some online prayer groups enforce confidentiality and kindness. Some theological forums require participants to summarise an opponent's argument fairly before responding. These practices are not mere etiquette. They reshape attention. They prevent outrage from becoming the default currency.

The difference between managed and unmanaged threads is stark. An unmanaged comment section beneath a viral clip often becomes a theatre of accusation. The strongest voices dominate. Sarcasm replaces argument. People arrive to win, not to understand. In a moderated space, the tone changes. People slow down. They ask questions. The presence of norms makes humility possible.

The motif threading this section is the spark. Outrage is a spark: quick, bright, contagious. It lights a room and burns it down. Communities need fire for warmth, but they also need hearths—structures that contain flame. Platforms distribute sparks. Communities must build hearths.

This raises a deeper point about authority. In the feed, the loudest disagreement is often mistaken for the most important. Controversy becomes a ranking signal. Leaders and influencers learn this quickly.

Some exploit it. Others are dragged into it. The abstraction "relevance" becomes a behaviour: responding publicly to every provocation to avoid seeming weak. The implication is exhaustion and constant conflict.

Ancient cautions about speech were designed to protect the community's capacity for attention. Gossip scatters attention. Division consumes it. In monastic settings, practices of silence and confession were not anti-social. They were anti-fragmentation. They prevented the community from becoming a swarm of competing narratives. Digital communities have few built-in equivalents.

So what practices might resist platform logics without denying the reality of disagreement? Begin with temporality. Outrage thrives on immediacy. Deliberate delay changes the field. A community that insists on waiting before responding—hours, days—reduces the reward of instant reaction. The behaviour is simple: not commenting immediately. Name the abstraction: restraint. Explain the mechanism: delay reduces amplification incentives. Implication: conflict becomes less performative.

Second, communities can privilege direct conversation over public performance. In many traditions, correction begins privately. Public rebuke is a last resort. Online, this order is inverted because public rebuke receives more attention. Reversing the order requires discipline. The behaviour is concrete: messaging privately, seeking clarification, asking consent before quoting. The implication is decreased spectacle.

Third, communities can demand interpretive charity as a norm. This is not naïveté. It is intellectual hygiene. It means reading an opponent's argument in its strongest plausible form. It also means distinguishing between error and malice. Platforms blur this distinction because outrage treats both as equally profitable.

A credible limitation appears here. Moderation and norms can become tools of control. "Civility" has sometimes been used to silence marginal voices or to protect abusive power. The reconciliation is transparency and shared governance. Norms must be explicit. Moderators must be accountable. Rules must protect the vulnerable, not merely the comfortable. A moderated forum that demands politeness while allowing harm is not a hearth; it is a velvet cage.

Return to the "angry" reaction as a ranking signal. The platform measures emotion. It cannot measure the moral quality of that emotion. There are times when anger is appropriate—against injustice, cruelty, exploitation. The question is not whether anger is wrong. The question is whether anger is being harnessed for formation or for spectacle. A community that cannot express anger may be complacent. A community that cannot express anything else becomes addicted.

The forward tension is therefore not a call for perpetual calm. It is a call for communities to reclaim agency over their emotional economy. Who sets the pace of your disagreements—the platform or your values? Who benefits when you fight publicly? Who is harmed when you do?

The section ends with a diagnostic question that looks ahead to the chapter's final movement. When you find yourself pulled into digital conflict around belief, do you feel more faithful afterwards, or merely more certain? Platforms can give certainty cheaply. Communities need truth, which is slower and more costly. The next pages explore what it might mean to inhabit digital spaces with different rules—rules that reward listening over sparks.

Digital Spaces with Different Rules

On 17 March 2020, in Oxford, the Church of England authorised clergy to conduct services remotely as public worship was suspended in response to COVID-19 restrictions. Within weeks, countless parishes were streaming liturgy on Facebook Live, hosting small groups on Zoom, and sending pastoral letters by email. Some efforts were frantic. Others were quietly inventive. One parish began holding a short evening prayer each weekday on Zoom, limited to thirty participants, with microphones muted for the psalms and a deliberate minute of silence after the reading. The priest did not preach. People listened. Attendance stabilised. When in-person worship returned, the Zoom prayer continued, now joined by the housebound and the geographically distant. The digital space did not replace the parish. It became a second doorway.

Five words belong here. *The room learned new rules.*

The question at the end of this chapter is not whether communities will inhabit digital spaces. They already do. The question is whether they will inhabit those spaces as tenants—accepting the landlord's logic of speed, performance, and engagement—or as builders who design different norms. Platforms are not neutral. They shape attention by default. Yet digital life is not limited to platforms that reward outrage and visibility. Communities can choose tools, formats, and rituals that cultivate different outcomes.

Begin with the most basic fact about the feed: it is optimised for *continuation*. The next post arrives instantly. The scroll never ends. Time dissolves. In such an environment, listening becomes difficult because listening requires closure: one voice at a time, a beginning and an end. The abstraction "attention" becomes visible behaviour: staying with one thing rather than switching. The implication is clear. If a community wants depth, it must shape time.

This is why experiments in slower, smaller gatherings matter. Their strength is not technological sophistication. It is constraint. Limiting group size changes the moral atmosphere. Thirty people can recognise each other. Three hundred cannot. A livestream with thousands of viewers is a broadcast; a call with twenty people is a gathering. The difference is not sentiment. It is accountability. In smaller spaces, absence is noticed. In larger spaces, absence is invisible.

A second named example illustrates intentional design. In March 2020, the Vatican's daily Mass livestreams drew large audiences, but many local communities began experimenting with small digital groups alongside the broadcasts. A Jesuit parish in London, for instance, used Zoom for structured evening prayer while maintaining recorded homilies for broader reach. Show the behaviour: separating broadcast teaching from interactive gathering. Name the abstraction: belonging. Explain the mechanism: different formats serve different communal goods. Implication: communities can use digital reach without collapsing into pure performance.

Performance is the central danger of digital religion. Platforms reward those who speak well on camera, who frame messages sharply, who produce content consistently. These are skills. They are not identical to pastoral wisdom or communal care. Rituals that encourage listening over performance counterbalance this pressure. Silence is one such ritual. Silence is not the absence of content; it is a refusal to fill space with noise. In digital settings, silence can feel awkward, and awkwardness is precisely why it matters. Awkwardness interrupts the entertainment expectation.

Another ritual is the deliberate rotation of voice. In many traditions, the same few people dominate speech by default. Online, dominance can become absolute because those who speak quickly and confidently take the floor. Some groups have adopted structured turn-taking: a short reading, then each person speaks for one minute, then microphones are muted again. The behaviour is concrete: time limits and muting. Name the abstraction: equality. Explain the mechanism: constraints prevent charismatic capture. Implication: quieter members become participants rather than spectators.

These practices resemble older forms of communal discipline. Monastic rules, Quaker meetings, and synagogue liturgies all include structures that govern speech and silence. They were designed to protect attention and prevent domination. Digital communities can borrow this wisdom without imitation. The aim is not to create a museum of piety. It is to build a room where the platform's default incentives do not set the tone.

A credible limitation must be acknowledged. Digital spaces can never fully replicate embodied gathering. Bodies carry information screens cannot: fatigue, grief, shared laughter, the subtle trust built by physical presence. There are also inequities: access to stable internet, private space, and time. The reconciliation is hybrid practice. Hybrid does not mean streaming a service and calling it community. It means linking online and offline in ways that reinforce responsibility.

Hybrid practice becomes most convincing when it produces tangible care. An online group that prays together and then coordinates meals for a member recovering from surgery is not merely a digital chat. It is a community using digital tools to organise embodied action. The abstraction "solidarity" becomes visible behaviour: meals delivered, visits arranged, costs shared. The implication is that digital gathering can support material care rather than replacing it.

The motif threading this section is the hearth. A hearth is not merely warmth; it is containment. It allows fire without destruction. Digital spaces need hearths because the surrounding landscape is windy: outrage, distraction, and performative debate are always available. A hearth requires boundaries. Boundaries can be temporal—meeting at a fixed time rather than existing in a constant thread. They can be spatial—using closed groups rather than open comment sections. They can be relational—membership by invitation and mutual commitment rather than by algorithmic discovery.

Moderation is part of hearth-building. The previous section contrasted unmanaged comment threads with moderated forums. Here the emphasis shifts from policing to cultivation. Moderation is not only removing harm. It is shaping tone. Some groups appoint facilitators whose role is to invite quieter voices, slow down reactive exchanges, and remind members of shared norms. The behaviour is simple: naming when conversation becomes performative. Name the abstraction: integrity. Explain the mechanism: gentle intervention shifts incentives from winning to understanding. Implication: disagreement becomes less viral but more honest.

Tool choice also matters. Platforms designed for broadcasting will encourage performance. Tools designed for collaboration and smaller groups will encourage participation. Email lists, private forums, group calls, and encrypted messaging each shape community differently. The point is not technological purity. It is alignment between tool and purpose.

A further tension appears. Digital spaces tempt communities to scale. Scale looks like success. Numbers reassure. Yet many forms of care do not scale easily without changing nature. A pastor can know thirty people's stories deeply. Knowing three thousand requires delegation and systematisation. That can be done well. It can also become managerial. Communities must decide what they mean by growth: more viewers, or deeper belonging?

This returns us to the opening parish with its weekday Zoom prayer. Its success was not measured by virality. It was measured by steadiness. People returned. They were noticed. The format created a rhythm that resisted the feed. The room had rules: silence, limited numbers, shared speech. These rules did not feel efficient. They felt faithful to the kind of community the parish wanted to be.

The forward test at the chapter's end is therefore diagnostic. When you participate in digital community around belief, what is being rewarded—your presence or your performance? Are you invited to listen, or pressured to react? Are you known, or merely counted? Digital spaces can host genuine community, but only when communities accept the cost of building hearths: constraints, norms, and slower rhythms that refuse to let the platform's weather decide what kind of people they become.

Chapter 8
Conscience in a Scored World

At 9.00 a.m. on a Monday morning, a manager opens a dashboard before speaking to a colleague. The screen displays coloured bars, percentile ranks, trend arrows, and a single composite score. It compresses a year of labour into a handful of numbers. Only after this silent consultation does the conversation begin. The exchange feels courteous, even humane, yet something decisive has already happened. Judgement has been framed in advance, shaped by a system that translates effort, character, and potential into metrics that can be compared, archived, and acted upon. No accusation has been made. No praise has been spoken. Still, a moral atmosphere has settled over the room.

Scenes like this are no longer confined to corporate life. Students encounter them through learning platforms that track engagement and predict attainment. Drivers meet them in insurance apps that reward or penalise behaviour. Parents glimpse them in school portals. Workers see them in performance reviews and productivity tools. Even leisure is scored: steps counted, sleep graded, moods tracked. The result is not merely more information. It is a new environment for conscience, one in which worth appears measurable and moral standing feels permanently provisional.

Conscience has never existed in a vacuum. It is formed by practices, stories, expectations, and communities. Yet the texture of moral self-understanding changes when judgement arrives continuously, impersonally, and at scale. Dashboards do not shout. They whisper, persistently, that value is visible, that comparison is normal, and that improvement is always possible if one aligns with the right indicators. This chapter turns inward to ask what happens to conscience under such pressure. Not in theory. In daily life.

Earlier chapters traced how algorithms guide decisions, shape communities, and rearrange authority. Here the focus narrows. What kind of moral agents are we becoming when our actions are constantly translated into scores? How does the habit of being ranked affect imagination, responsibility, and mercy? These questions are not abstract. They surface whenever someone thinks, *The system required it*, or *I followed the policy*, or *The data made the choice clear*. They surface when discomfort is numbed by compliance.

The first movement of this chapter examines the quiet power of comparison. Scoring systems do not merely evaluate outcomes; they teach us what counts. Achievement dashboards echo older ideas of merit and worthiness, yet with a crucial difference. Where earlier moral frameworks were mediated by narrative, ritual, and judgement exercised face to face, digital scoring systems offer immediate feedback without explanation. The moral imagination narrows. Good becomes what is measured. Failure becomes what is visible. The danger is not ambition itself, but the gradual replacement of discernment with optimisation.

From there, the chapter turns to a subtler temptation: the outsourcing of ethics. Automated filters, compliance checklists, and risk calculators promise safety and consistency. They also offer relief. If a system approves an action, responsibility feels lighter. If a policy permits it, conscience rests. Yet history is crowded with examples of harm committed in the name of procedure. When judgement is displaced entirely onto systems, moral agency atrophies. The chapter does not argue against rules or safeguards. It insists that they cannot carry the full weight of ethical life.

Against this backdrop, older practices return with fresh relevance. Many traditions have cultivated forms of examination of conscience precisely because human beings drift. These practices were never about tallying infractions alone. They were about attention: noticing where time went, whom one ignored, what one justified too easily. Updating such practices for digital life does not require nostalgia. It requires honesty about data trails, attention economies, and complicity in systems that reward harm at a distance. The question is not whether one is pure. It is whether one is awake.

The chapter's final movement resists both despair and grandiosity. Conscience is not restored by heroic gestures. It is shaped by habits. Small ones. Repeatable ones. Habits that slow judgement, reopen empathy, and make space for mercy. A device-free evening. Shared reflection rather than solitary optimisation. Deliberate acts that interrupt score-based logic by attending to those who cannot repay or be ranked. These practices do not reject technology. They refuse to let it define the limits of moral concern.

A quiet motif runs through the chapter: softness. Not weakness, but responsiveness. A soft conscience is one that remains permeable to surprise, correction, and compassion. Scored environments tend to harden us, rewarding defensiveness and performance. The work of conscience, then, is not to become flawless but to remain human under pressure.

This chapter does not offer a new moral code. It sharpens perception. It asks readers to notice when judgement is being delegated, when comparison is shaping self-worth, and when compliance is masquerading as virtue. It invites a slower reckoning, one that neither panics nor shrugs. The aim is modest and demanding at once: to recover the capacity to say, with clarity and humility, *I am responsible*, even when systems are involved.

The pages that follow move from dashboards to decisions, from policies to persons, from scores to stories. They ask what it means to form a conscience that can live honestly in a world that measures relentlessly. Not by fleeing the scored world, but by refusing to let it have the final word.

Dashboards of Worthiness

In November 2013, at Microsoft's headquarters in Redmond, Washington, senior leaders announced the end of a controversial performance management practice known internally as "stack ranking". For years, employees had been scored and sorted into forced distributions, with clear winners and losers, regardless of absolute performance. The decision to abandon the system followed mounting internal criticism and external reporting that linked the rankings to anxiety, risk aversion, and corrosive competition. The outcome was concrete: bonuses and promotions were decoupled from rigid percentile scores, and managers were told to evaluate contribution more holistically. Yet the episode left a residue. Many employees had already internalised the logic of being continuously measured against peers. The dashboard had trained them.

That training matters. A performance review is not only an administrative tool. It is a moral signal. It tells people what is worth striving for, what counts as failure, and how much of themselves is visible to authority. When such judgements are rendered through dashboards—colour-coded, quantified, and compared—they do more than summarise behaviour. They reshape imagination. They teach people how to see themselves.

The modern workplace is saturated with these instruments. Objectives and Key Results, engagement scores, productivity trackers, customer ratings, peer feedback graphs. Each promises clarity. Each claims neutrality. Together, they form a moral environment in which worth appears legible and portable. This is not new in spirit. Societies have long ranked, rewarded, and excluded. What is new is the intimacy and frequency of the judgement. Scores update weekly, sometimes daily. Comparison is automated. Memory is permanent.

To see the effect, consider the ordinary ritual of an annual performance review. A manager opens a portal. On the screen are metrics: sales closed, tickets resolved, deadlines met, targets missed. A percentile rank sits nearby, anchoring interpretation. The manager may know the employee well. They may value qualities not captured by the system: mentoring, judgement under pressure, restraint. Yet the numbers speak first. They frame the conversation before a word is exchanged. This is the *show*. The *name* follows easily: performance, contribution, potential. The *explanation* appeals to fairness and consistency. The *implication* is rarely examined: a person's moral standing within the organisation is increasingly mediated by abstractions they did not choose.

Constant comparison alters how people judge themselves. When every action feeds a metric, attention shifts from meaning to optimisation. One begins to ask not *Was this right?* but *Will this count?* The distinction matters. Moral imagination requires the capacity to weigh competing goods, to tolerate ambiguity, to act without immediate reward. Dashboards reward clarity and speed. They compress complex activity into simplified signals that travel well across systems. In doing so, they privilege what can be counted over what must be discerned.

Older traditions of merit were slower and thicker. Whether in religious orders, guilds, or civic institutions, worthiness was assessed through narrative, apprenticeship, and reputation. A novice was observed over time. Failures were contextualised. Growth was expected to be uneven. Judgement was public but personal, exercised by people who knew the candidate's story. These systems were hardly benign; they excluded and disciplined. Yet they acknowledged, at least implicitly, that virtue could not be read off a ledger.

Dashboards revive the language of merit while stripping it of context. Achievement becomes portable. Worth becomes comparative by default. A score of 4.2 is meaningful only against other scores. The moral horizon narrows. One is good *relative to peers*, not in relation to shared purposes or obligations. This is a quiet shift, but a profound one. It trains conscience to seek validation externally, continuously, and competitively.

There is evidence that such environments change behaviour. Studies of performance measurement in organisations have shown that employees adjust effort toward what is measured, even when those measures capture only part of the task. Christopher Hood's work on audit cultures, published in the early 2000s, documented how targets intended to improve accountability often distorted practice, encouraging gaming and risk avoidance. The behaviour is visible: teachers teach to the test; clinicians prioritise measurable outcomes; workers choose safe projects that score well. The abstraction of *efficiency* becomes a set of decisions that quietly displace care.

A counter-example is often raised. Metrics, it is argued, can expose bias and protect against arbitrary judgement. Transparent criteria can limit favouritism. Data can surface patterns of discrimination that anecdote hides. This is true, and it matters. In 2018, for example, several UK public bodies used performance data to identify pay gaps and promotion disparities that subjective assessment had normalised. Numbers can correct blindness. They can discipline power.

The reconciliation lies in recognising the difference between *using* measures and *being formed* by them. When dashboards are treated as provisional tools, open to challenge and supplemented by judgement, they can serve justice. When they become the primary language of worth, they begin to colonise conscience. The problem is not measurement itself. It is the silent moral pedagogy that accompanies ubiquitous scoring.

This pedagogy reaches beyond work. Fitness apps grade activity. Social platforms count approval. Credit systems rate trustworthiness. Each translates a dimension of life into a scale that invites comparison. Each claims to describe reality while subtly prescribing behaviour. The abstraction of *trust* becomes a numerical threshold. The abstraction of *risk* becomes a colour-coded warning. Decisions follow. Conscience learns to defer.

A quiet motif runs through these systems: the mirror. Dashboards present a reflection, but it is a selective one. They show what the system can see. Over time, people begin to act for the mirror. They curate themselves toward the indicators that return praise. Qualities that resist quantification—patience, mercy, courage to dissent—fade from view. Not because they vanish, but because they no longer appear to matter.

There are limits to this effect. Not all scoring environments flatten moral life. Some organisations deliberately resist totalisation. They use metrics sparingly, review them in conversation, and make space for narrative judgement. In such settings, the dashboard remains a reference, not a verdict. The visible behaviour is different: managers override scores, teams discuss trade-offs, leaders explain decisions that defy the numbers. The metric is named as partial. The implication is clear: conscience still has room to breathe.

Yet the broader cultural current flows the other way. Scored systems promise relief from uncertainty. They offer the comfort of alignment: if the indicators are green, one has done well. This comfort is seductive. It dulls the discomfort that often signals moral work. When everything important is measured, nothing important needs to be wrestled with. That is the risk.

The formation of conscience depends on friction. It grows through encounters with limits, with claims that cannot be satisfied simultaneously, with demands that resist optimisation. Dashboards reduce friction by design. They smooth judgement into gradients. They invite incremental improvement rather than qualitative reflection. Over time, this can produce a brittle moral self: highly responsive to feedback, yet anxious, defensive, and hesitant to act beyond the frame.

The closing question of this section is not whether dashboards will disappear. They will not. It is whether they will remain instruments, or become arbiters. When a score conflicts with a story, which carries weight? When a metric rewards harm done efficiently, who notices? The forward test is simple to state and hard to live: the next time a dashboard defines worth, what would it take to pause, to ask what it cannot see, and to let conscience speak before the numbers decide?

Outsourcing Ethics to Systems

On 8 August 2013, in Amsterdam, the District Court of Amsterdam ruled that the "Legal Intelligence" system used by the travel website Booking.com to rank and display hotels had misled consumers by creating an impression of objective ordering while incorporating commercial factors. The court's language was specific: the presentation of results implied neutrality where there was none. The decision did not accuse the platform of hating its customers. It identified a familiar modern manoeuvre: hiding moral and commercial choices behind procedures that look like compliance. The outcome was a legal rebuke, but the deeper lesson is broader. Systems can become alibis.

Five words belong here. *The policy became a shield.*

The temptation to outsource ethics is not primarily a temptation to be wicked. It is a temptation to be relieved. Ethical reflection is costly. It requires time, uncertainty, and the willingness to bear responsibility for imperfect decisions. Automated tools promise to remove that burden. A filter flags prohibited content. A risk calculator assigns a score. A compliance checklist confirms that required steps have been taken. The person using the tool can then say, with a clean conscience, "I followed the process."

Show the behaviour. A moderator removes a post because an automated system flagged it. Name the abstraction: fairness. Explain the mechanism: automation promises consistent enforcement. Implication: the human agent feels absolved, even when the outcome is unjust.

This dynamic appears across domains. In workplaces, ethics training often ends with a quiz. Pass the quiz, and one is "compliant." In finance, risk controls are encoded in thresholds: if the indicator stays within bounds, the activity is deemed acceptable. In healthcare administration, triage decisions can be guided by scoring systems. In social media, "community standards" are enforced partly by classifiers that detect patterns of hate speech, nudity, or violence. In each case, the system offers a procedural substitute for judgement.

The substitute feels attractive because it is legible. Judgement is hard to audit. A checklist can be audited. A score can be logged. A workflow can be proved. Organisations love proof. It protects them from lawsuits and from reputational damage. Individuals love proof too. It protects them from inner discomfort. Conscience becomes a compliance function.

This is why the phrase "I was just following policy" remains so potent. It does not need algorithms to exist. Bureaucracy has long offered moral insulation. Hannah Arendt's analysis of the "banality of evil" was precisely about ordinary people performing harm through routine, not through overt malice. The modern twist is that algorithms make routine more persuasive. When a decision is produced by a system, it feels less personal and therefore less morally fraught. The output carries the tone of inevitability.

Consider content moderation again. Platforms must remove certain content quickly: child exploitation, incitement to violence, explicit threats. Automated detection can help reduce harm. This is the credible counter-example that must be honoured. Systems can protect. They can help humans scale moral action. The reconciliation lies in distinguishing between *automation as support* and *automation as absolution*. The first expands care. The second replaces it.

Absolution through compliance appears most clearly when rules are treated as the limit of responsibility. A company may meet formal requirements while ignoring foreseeable harm. The behaviour is visible: pointing to a policy document when challenged. Name the abstraction: responsibility. Explain the mechanism: legal compliance is confused with moral adequacy. Implication: harm is externalised as someone else's problem.

A widely discussed case illustrates this structure even when the details differ by industry. In the years before the 2008 financial crisis, many institutions relied on credit ratings and internal risk models to justify exposure to complex mortgage-backed securities. When challenged, they often pointed to ratings and compliance procedures. The instruments said the risk was acceptable. The systems had signed off. When the collapse came, many actors claimed surprise. The moral failure was not only miscalculation. It was outsourcing judgement to tools that could not carry the ethical weight of the decisions being made.

The same pattern plays out at smaller scales. A company deploys an automated hiring tool that screens applicants. It claims neutrality because it uses "data". Later, evidence emerges that the system disadvantages certain groups. The company responds by pointing to vendor documentation and internal policies. It insists it followed best practice. The system becomes a shield against responsibility. Yet the harm remains. People were excluded. Lives were altered.

To see the mechanics, follow the Show → Name → Explain → Implication engine closely. Show: an applicant receives an automated rejection within minutes, without explanation or appeal. Name: efficiency. Explain: automated screening reduces costs and speeds hiring. Implication: the cost is transferred to applicants who cannot contest decisions and to societies that inherit unjust distribution of opportunity.

Now extend the logic to risk calculators. Many institutions use scoring systems to determine eligibility for services—loans, insurance, housing, benefits. These scores may be predictive. They may also encode historical inequities. When a person is denied, the institution can claim impartiality: "the system applied the criteria." Yet criteria are chosen. Variables are weighted. Thresholds are set. Moral agency has been exercised. It has simply been buried.

The phrase "checklists cannot replace judgement" can sound like a slogan. To make it real, pair it with behaviour. Judgement appears when someone asks, "What outcome are we producing for the person on the other end?" Judgement appears when someone overrides the system and documents why. Judgement appears when an organisation creates appeals and reviews error rates, rather than treating automated outputs as final. Judgement appears when the reasons for decisions can be explained in language a non-specialist can understand.

Ethical outsourcing thrives in opacity. If a system cannot be challenged, it cannot be corrected. This is why transparency matters—not because everything must be public, but because accountability requires that someone can trace a decision back to reasons. When reasons disappear, power becomes faceless. Faceless power invites abdication: "It wasn't me."

The motif threading this section is the mask. Systems can mask intent, not always deliberately, but effectively. A ranking algorithm masks commercial preference as relevance. A compliance checklist masks moral deliberation as a completed form. A risk score masks judgement as prediction. Masks are useful when protection is needed. They are dangerous when they enable harm without recognition.

There is also a psychological dimension. People experience "moral licensing": the sense that doing something approved grants permission to ignore other concerns. Passing compliance training can feel like becoming ethical. Using a "responsible AI" tool can feel like having addressed bias. These tools can be helpful. They can also become talismans—objects that ward off guilt while leaving underlying practices unchanged.

The antidote is not perfectionism. It is responsibility that stays close to consequences. Responsibility is not merely a policy posture. It is a willingness to remain answerable when systems err. It is also a willingness to admit that some ethical questions cannot be reduced to thresholds. A content filter can detect prohibited words. It cannot detect context reliably. A risk score can predict correlation. It cannot assign moral desert.

This leads to the final tension. As automated tools proliferate, the ease of outsourcing will grow. The systems will look more sophisticated. The documentation will look more reassuring. Organisations will be tempted to treat "compliance" as the end of moral thinking rather than its beginning. Individuals will be tempted to treat "the system said" as a way to avoid the discomfort of agency.

The forward test is therefore blunt. When you next rely on a tool that claims to protect you ethically—a policy, a filter, a checklist, a score—ask what it allows you to *stop noticing*. Ask whose cost disappears when you accept its output without question. Then decide whether you are using the system, or whether you are hiding behind it.

Updating Examination of Conscience

In April 2010, Google launched a tool that would later be known as "Google Takeout", allowing users to download an archive of data associated with their accounts. For many, the first download was unsettling. Search queries, location traces, YouTube watch history, contacts, photos, calendar entries—years of life rendered as files. The outcome was not a scandal in the newspaper. It was a private shock: the discovery that one's ordinary days had left a long, legible trail.

Five words belong here. *Your life became retrievable.*

Traditions of examination of conscience were developed for exactly this sort of shock, though their founders could not have imagined the infrastructure. Examination is a practice of moral accounting—not the sterile accounting of dashboards, but the humane work of attention. It asks: What did I love? What did I neglect? Where did I act with courage, and where did I hide? It assumes that people drift, justify, and forget, and that without deliberate reflection the soul becomes shaped by forces it does not see.

Digital life introduces new forces, and it makes certain old ones louder. The most obvious is attention itself. Attention is no longer merely the capacity to focus; it is a contested resource. Platforms measure it, sell it, and train it. This means that moral formation now happens not only through choices about behaviour but through choices about *where the mind rests*. A person who spends hours consuming content designed to provoke anxiety will not only think different thoughts; they will become a different kind of thinker. The abstraction "character" becomes visible behaviour: what you repeatedly attend to when no one is watching.

Updating examination of conscience for digital life is therefore not moral panic about screens. It is refusing to treat attention as ethically neutral. It is also refusing to treat data trails as merely technical. Trails record desire. They expose habit. They reveal patterns of avoidance and fixation. In older forms of examination, one reviewed the day's actions and intentions. In digital life, a parallel review can include the traces one leaves behind—not to indulge self-surveillance, but to make drift visible.

The first step is conceptual: to recognise that digital choices are moral choices because they distribute time, attention, and social impact. Even small clicks contribute to larger systems. A search query trains autocomplete. A view contributes to recommendation signals. A share amplifies. The individual act feels tiny. The aggregation is not. This is where complicity enters—not as melodrama, but as ordinary participation in systems that can reward harm while appearing harmless.

Show the behaviour. A person watches a sensational clip and the platform recommends more extreme content. Name the abstraction: complicity. Explain the mechanism: engagement signals shape distribution. Implication: moral responsibility includes what one sustains through attention, not only what one actively endorses.

Two named examples sharpen this without inventing drama. First, in 2016, the United States presidential election revealed how social media platforms could be used for large-scale manipulation through targeted content and coordinated influence operations; investigations and academic work since have documented how engagement-driven ranking can amplify divisive material. Second, in 2018, the publication of the "Facebook Files" and subsequent reporting highlighted internal awareness that certain kinds of content—especially emotionally charged posts—were boosted by engagement metrics. The details of these controversies matter less here than the structural point: platforms measure what we do, and our doing helps determine what others see.

Now introduce the credible limitation. Individuals cannot carry the full moral burden of systemic design. It is neither fair nor psychologically healthy to treat every click as a cosmic referendum. The reconciliation lies in scale-appropriate responsibility. Examination of conscience is not a demand to purify oneself from the modern world. It is an invitation to reclaim agency where agency exists: in patterns, not perfection; in awareness, not obsession.

The motif threading this section is the ledger. Traditional examinations often used the language of accounting: debts, forgiveness, restitution. Digital life produces literal ledgers—logs, histories, archives. These ledgers can become instruments of shame if treated as proof of a fixed self. They can also become tools for truth if treated as evidence of habit. The question is what one does with the record.

An updated examination might begin, as older ones did, with gratitude: what gave life today? But it must also include questions that match the new terrain. Not frantic questions, but precise ones. Where did my attention go when I was tired? Which voices did I allow to shape my mood? What did I reward with my clicks? What did I avoid by scrolling? Whom did I reduce to a label? Whose suffering did I treat as content?

These questions become sharper when paired with data. Reviewing one's own data trail is not a stunt. It is a form of honest observation. One might open screen-time reports, browsing histories, or location timelines and notice patterns: the late-night spiral into news; the repeated return to certain forms of outrage; the absence of time spent on purposeful reading or sustained conversation. The behaviour is concrete: opening the report rather than guessing. Name the abstraction: honesty. Explain the mechanism: externalised records expose self-deception. Implication: moral reflection becomes grounded rather than sentimental.

There is risk here. Data trails can encourage self-judgement that is harsh or reductive. Numbers can colonise conscience rather than serve it. That danger is real, and it mirrors the earlier problem of dashboards of worthiness. The reconciliation is interpretive. The purpose is not to score oneself but to see oneself. A ledger is not the same as a verdict.

Traditions of examination also emphasised intention. Digital environments complicate intention because they are designed to capture attention regardless of intention. A person may open an app for one purpose and end up elsewhere. This does not eliminate responsibility, but it does change the kind of responsibility required. It demands humility about vulnerability to design. It also demands practical wisdom: setting boundaries, choosing contexts, recognising triggers. These are not life hacks; they are moral protections.

Community matters here as well. In many traditions, examination is not purely private. Confession, spiritual direction, and communal accountability exist because self-perception is unreliable. Digital life increases the need for such mirrors, not decreases it. Algorithms already mirror us, but they mirror appetite, not wisdom. Human community can mirror values. The behaviour is tangible: discussing patterns with a trusted friend, mentor, or group rather than confessing to a dashboard. Name the abstraction: accountability. Explain the mechanism: mutual recognition corrects self-deception. Implication: conscience remains relational rather than solitary.

Updating examination of conscience also requires naming complicity without theatrics. One cannot avoid using systems that are woven into work, education, and social life. Yet one can notice where participation becomes endorsement. Sharing a rumour is not neutral. Laughing at dehumanising memes is not neutral. Consuming content that thrives on humiliation is not neutral. The moral question is not "Am I online?" but "What kind of person am I becoming through my online habits, and what kind of world do those habits reward?"

This is where older spiritual language remains useful. Many traditions speak of *formation*—the gradual shaping of desire through repeated practices. Algorithms accelerate formation by repeating stimuli. The feed becomes a liturgy of sorts: repeated gestures, repeated words, repeated rewards. Examination of conscience is a counter-liturgy: a practice that interrupts automaticity and reintroduces reflection.

The section ends, appropriately, on a forward test rather than a tidy resolution. The next time you are tempted to treat your digital trail as either irrelevant or shameful, treat it instead as information about your loves. Then ask a question that no dashboard can answer: if your attention is your offering, what altar have you been feeding, and what would it look like to redirect that offering—deliberately, quietly, and without performance?

Habits that Keep Hearts Soft

On a Tuesday evening in February 2019, in a semi-detached house in Reading, the Patel family did something unremarkable and quietly radical. At 6.30 p.m., they placed their phones in a kitchen drawer. Not forever. Not with speeches. Just for the evening. The outcome was not transcendence. It was awkward silence, mild irritation, then conversation. By the third week, the drawer no longer felt like deprivation. It felt like relief.

Softness returned slowly.

Habits that keep conscience supple are rarely dramatic. They work against the grain of a culture that rewards intensity, visibility, and optimisation. Their power lies in repetition and modesty. Where algorithmic systems harden judgement through scoring, ranking, and constant comparison, these habits cultivate what older traditions called *discernment*: the capacity to notice, to pause, to respond rather than react. They are not about withdrawal from modern life but about reintroducing texture where life has become smooth.

The first habit is restraint, often described as sabbath. Sabbath is not merely rest. It is structured refusal. It draws a boundary around time and declares that productivity is not the highest good. In a digital context, sabbath from devices is visible behaviour: choosing periods when notifications remain unanswered and feeds unopened. The abstraction is trust. The explanation is simple: if the world collapses without constant monitoring, then we were never in control to begin with. The implication is profound. Restraint interrupts the illusion that worth depends on responsiveness.

Historical grounding matters here. In the Jewish tradition, sabbath observance has persisted for millennia precisely because it resists instrumentalisation. In 2015, sociologist Judith Shulevitz described sabbath as a "technology of freedom," not because it rejects tools but because it limits their claims. The same logic applies now. A weekly device sabbath does not solve systemic problems, but it retrains desire. It teaches the nervous system that absence is survivable.

The limitation must be named. Not everyone can disconnect easily. Care workers, shift workers, and those in precarious employment may find such practices costly. The reconciliation is scale and creativity. Sabbath is not an all-or-nothing commandment. It can be an hour, an evening, a morning. The moral weight lies not in duration but in intentionality.

The second habit is shared reflection. Algorithms offer mirrors that reflect behaviour but not meaning. Shared reflection introduces interpretation. It takes place in families, friendship circles, congregations, or small groups. The behaviour is concrete: speaking aloud about how technology shapes one's mood, priorities, and patience. The abstraction is humility. The explanation follows: speaking dissolves the fantasy of solitary mastery. The implication is relational conscience, one that is corrected and encouraged by others.

Two examples sharpen this. In 2017, the Benedict Option discussion groups that emerged in parts of the United States and Europe—whatever one thinks of their broader agenda—demonstrated that people were hungry for spaces to talk honestly about formation, distraction, and limits. More quietly, in 2020, during pandemic lockdowns, many mutual-aid groups held regular online check-ins that were not task-focused but reflective, creating shared language for fatigue and moral strain. These were not performance spaces. They were listening spaces.

The counter-example is performative vulnerability. Social platforms reward confessional disclosure without accountability. Reflection becomes content. The reconciliation is containment. Shared reflection requires boundaries: smaller groups, clearer norms, and resistance to broadcasting. Softness depends on safety.

The third habit is deliberate acts of mercy. Mercy sounds abstract until paired with behaviour. It is time given without metrics, attention offered without amplification, kindness without capture. In digital systems, almost every action is counted. Mercy is action that refuses counting. The abstraction is grace. The explanation is theological and practical: when everything is measured, unmeasured giving restores proportion. The implication is a conscience that remembers that not all value is visible.

Acts of mercy need not be heroic. They might include checking on a neighbour without posting about it, volunteering regularly rather than episodically, or choosing not to engage in public shaming even when it would be rewarded. In 2018, research by psychologist Paul Bloom on empathy and compassion suggested that sustainable moral action depends less on emotional intensity than on stable practices. Mercy, in this sense, is a habit, not a feeling.

Here too, a limitation arises. Mercy can be co-opted into self-congratulation. The reconciliation is secrecy. Many traditions insist that mercy loses something when advertised. This is not moral purity; it is protection of motive.

Threaded through these habits is a quiet motif: *thickness*. Algorithmic life tends towards thinness—fast judgements, compressed signals, reduced context. Habits that keep hearts soft reintroduce thickness: time that stretches, conversations that wander, actions that resist immediate feedback. Thickness is not nostalgia. It is resistance to reduction.

Return to the family in Reading. Their routine evolved. Evenings without devices became normal. They argued less about screen time because it was no longer constant. A child began reading again, not because of a rule but because boredom made space. No one tracked improvement. No dashboard marked success. The change held because it was shared and repeatable.

The unresolved tension remains. These habits operate at the personal and communal level, while the systems shaping life operate at scale. Soft hearts can feel fragile in hard structures. The forward test is not whether such habits fix the world, but whether they preserve something essential within it. As you consider the next small, repeatable step—an evening, a conversation, an unmeasured kindness—the question is simple and demanding: what would it mean to choose softness not as escape, but as preparation for living faithfully amid systems that prefer you efficient, visible, and scored?

Chapter 9
Practising Faith Online

At 7.00 a.m., a phone vibrates on a bedside table in Manchester. The notification is gentle, almost polite. It does not announce breaking news or demand an urgent reply. It says, simply, *breathe*. The app was installed during a difficult winter, at the suggestion of a friend. At first, the reminder felt artificial, a simulation of discipline. Months later, it has become a hinge in the day. Silence opens. Something real happens.

This is the quiet paradox of digital faith. Some of the most ancient human practices—prayer, meditation, study, confession—are now summoned by the same devices that deliver advertising, outrage, and distraction. A single screen mediates both noise and stillness. The question is no longer whether faith belongs online. It already lives there. The question is what kind of faith takes shape when its rhythms are nudged by notifications, tracked by streaks, and hosted on platforms designed for engagement rather than depth.

Practising faith has always involved tools. Scrolls, bells, candles, clocks, printed books: none of these were neutral, and each reshaped devotion in subtle ways. The printing press did not merely distribute scripture; it changed how individuals related to authority and interpretation. Mechanical clocks did not simply tell time; they reorganised prayer around hours rather than seasons. To notice that apps and streams shape spiritual life is not alarmism. It is historical literacy.

What *is* new is the density of mediation. Spiritual technologies now operate within an attention economy whose logic is constant feedback. Apps promise regularity. Streams promise access. Notifications promise help. And often, they deliver. A daily reminder can draw someone into silence who would otherwise drift past it. A livestreamed service can reconnect someone housebound or isolated. A shared reading plan can sustain commitment when energy wanes. These are not trivial goods. They matter because faith is embodied, habitual, and easily crowded out.

Yet the same systems that support regular practice also measure it. They count days, award badges, mark streaks, and offer dashboards of devotion. Subtly, the centre of gravity can shift. What began as a support for prayer becomes a performance of consistency. What began as an aid to discipline becomes a proxy for faithfulness. Older traditions warned against praying to be seen. Digital systems do not need spectators. They provide internalised ones.

This chapter sits at a delicate point in the book's arc. Much has been said already about authority, conscience, community, and personal formation under algorithmic pressure. Here, the focus narrows to practice. Not belief as abstraction, but belief enacted through repeated acts. The aim is neither to baptise technology nor to banish it. It is to cultivate judgement—an ability to choose tools that serve the soul rather than quietly reshape it.

The first movement of the chapter attends to rhythms. Apps, streams, and digital study tools promise something many people struggle to sustain: regularity. They externalise memory and motivation. In doing so, they can lower the threshold for practice. A daily reminder that opens into silence is not a gimmick; it is a scaffold. The deeper question is how scaffolds function over time. Do they support growth, or do they become load-bearing structures that cannot be removed without collapse?

From rhythms, the chapter turns to measurement. Streaks and badges are not morally neutral decorations. They encode values. They suggest that what matters most is continuity, visibility, and accumulation. This echoes much older anxieties within religious traditions about performed piety, about devotion shaped by external approval rather than internal orientation. The comparison between a quiet, unmeasured prayer and a logged session is not meant to romanticise the former or dismiss the latter. It is meant to sharpen awareness of motive. Why am I doing this? Who is it for? What would change if no one, including an app, noticed?

The argument is not that tracking always corrupts. For some, measurement sustains honesty. For others, it induces anxiety or competition. The point is discernment. A tool that strengthens practice for one person may hollow it out for another. Wisdom lies in noticing effects, not assuming intentions.

The chapter then widens again, exploring creativity rather than discipline. Digital spaces are not only sites of optimisation. They can host depth when used with care. New liturgies have emerged online, shaped by chat windows and shared silence. Online retreats have created temporary communities marked by attention rather than performance. Collaborative projects—shared prayer cycles, distributed study groups, collective lament—have found forms that would be difficult offline. These experiments matter because they resist the idea that technology inevitably flattens meaning. It does not. It amplifies what it is given.

A small, intentional online circle offers a glimpse of this possibility. Limited in size. Clear in purpose. Slow by design. Such spaces do not scale well, and that is precisely their strength. They trade reach for depth, metrics for presence. They remind us that digital does not have to mean mass, and that intimacy is not a function of proximity alone.

The final movement of the chapter is practical, but not prescriptive. Choosing tools that serve the soul requires asking different questions from those posed by app stores or marketing copy. Who owns this tool? What data does it collect? What behaviours does it reward? What does it assume about success? These questions are not technical trivia. They are moral inquiries. They locate spiritual practice within economies of attention, data, and profit, and ask whether alignment is possible.

The goal is not purity. No one practises faith outside systems. The goal is coherence. To choose tools whose design values do not quietly contradict one's deepest commitments. To accept help without surrendering agency. To use reminders without becoming ruled by them.

Throughout the chapter, a quiet motif recurs: *instrument or companion.* Is this technology an instrument I use, or a companion that shapes me? Instruments can be laid down. Companions form habits, expectations, and affections. The distinction is not always clear, and it shifts over time. But noticing the difference is itself a spiritual practice.

The questions raised here are not limited to any one tradition. They apply wherever people seek depth, meaning, and orientation amid digital saturation. They matter now because the default settings of most platforms pull in a different direction. They matter always because faith, however defined, lives or dies through practice.

As the chapter unfolds, the reader is invited neither to retreat nor to rush forward uncritically. Instead, the invitation is to slow down and look closely at the ordinary technologies already woven into daily devotion. To notice what they give. To notice what they ask in return. And to consider, with care and honesty, what it might mean to practise faith online without letting the logic of the platform become the logic of the soul.

Apps, Streams, and Sacred Rhythms

At 6.30 a.m. on a wet Tuesday in London, a small bell sounds from a phone on a kitchen counter. The sound is not an alarm. It is softer, almost shy. The notification comes from Headspace, the meditation app founded in London in 2010 by Andy Puddicombe, and on this particular morning in March 2019 it does something unexpectedly effective. The kettle waits. The message reads, *Take three minutes*. The phone is put face down. Silence begins.

This is not a conversion story. It is a scheduling story. And scheduling, for better or worse, has always been part of spiritual life. Monastic bells, prayer hours, fasting calendars, study cycles—none of these emerged by accident. They existed because intention alone proved unreliable. Habit needed help. So do we.

Five minutes change the day.

The surprise is not that a digital reminder can draw someone into silence. The surprise is that it works at all, given what else that same device does. The phone is a marketplace, a newsroom, a theatre, a ledger of obligations. Yet it is increasingly also a chapel, a study, a quiet room. Apps, streams, and notifications now mediate practices once anchored in place and community. This mediation deserves attention not because it is sinister, but because it is powerful.

Spiritual practice is rhythmic by nature. It repeats. It returns. It trains attention through ordinary faithfulness rather than dramatic insight. Digital tools enter precisely here, offering regularity where many people struggle to sustain it. The promise is modest and compelling: *we will remember for you.* In an age of fractured schedules and dispersed communities, this offer has real force.

Consider the Bible app YouVersion, launched by Life.Church in Oklahoma in 2008 and widely adopted by 2011. By design, it does something ancient in a modern way. It assigns daily readings, sends reminders, and tracks completion. For people without a local study group or fixed devotional hour, this structure can mean the difference between intention and practice. The abstraction of "discipline" becomes a visible behaviour: a passage read, a day marked complete.

The same pattern appears across traditions. Prayer apps prompt fixed hours. Meditation platforms schedule sessions. Online courses pace study over weeks rather than overwhelming the learner at once. The visible metric is not mystical attainment but attendance. Show up. Begin again.

Name the mechanism and it becomes clearer. These tools externalise memory. They shift the burden of recall from the individual to the system. Explain the effect and the benefit sharpens. External memory lowers friction. It reduces the cognitive cost of beginning. The implication is practical rather than theological: more people practise more often.

This is not trivial. Sociological studies of habit formation consistently show that regular cues increase adherence, even when motivation fluctuates. BJ Fogg's work on behaviour design, popularised in the late 2010s, emphasised small prompts tied to existing routines. Spiritual apps borrow this insight without advertising it. The bell replaces the monastery clock. The calendar notification replaces the parish noticeboard.

The motif here is the bell.

Bells do not pray. They call.

Historically, this was understood. In Benedictine monasteries, the bell marked the hour, not the quality of attention. The monks still had to show up. Digital bells function similarly, at least at first. They do not create devotion. They create an opening.

Streams extend this logic from time to place. Livestreamed services, recorded lectures, and guided practices dissolve geographical constraints. A commuter listens to morning prayer on a train. A night-shift worker joins a service after midnight. Access widens. The visible metric is reach: a stream viewed, a session joined.

The benefits are evident. During periods of crisis—pandemics, conflict, displacement—streams have sustained communal rhythms when physical gathering was impossible. The question is not whether this matters. It does. The question is what else changes when access becomes frictionless.

Here a limitation emerges. When practice is always available, it can become optional in a new way. Scarcity once carried weight. If prayer happened at a fixed hour in a fixed place, missing it meant something. When everything is replayable, postponement carries less cost. The counter-example matters because it complicates the narrative of pure gain.

This tension is not unique to digital tools. Printed books once raised similar anxieties. When scripture moved from communal hearing to private reading, some feared fragmentation and selective attention. Both happened. So did renewal. The reconciliation lies in recognising that tools amplify existing tendencies. They do not dictate outcomes.

Trust follows design.

Trust, here, is not an abstraction. It shows up as reliance. Do I rely on this reminder to begin, or does it replace an internal rhythm I am no longer cultivating? The behaviour is observable. When the notification fails, does practice collapse?

The answer varies. For some, digital scaffolding strengthens internal habits over time. For others, it becomes load-bearing. The difference often lies in how the tool is framed. Is it a temporary aid or a permanent prosthesis?

A second named example sharpens the picture. In 2016, the meditation app Calm, founded in San Francisco in 2012, began integrating sleep stories and timed reminders. The design goal was continuity. Users were encouraged to return nightly. The metric was retention. The benefit was obvious: better sleep routines reported in user surveys cited by Calm in 2019. The risk was quieter: practice drifting towards consumption, where listening replaced active attention.

This is not a moral failing. It is a design trade-off.

Efficiency always costs something.

Efficiency here means reduced effort. The visible behaviour is ease of entry. The implication is ambivalent. Ease can invite depth by removing barriers. It can also flatten experience by smoothing away resistance, which many traditions treat as formative.

The bell rings again.

At this point, a credible counter-example deserves space. There are practitioners who reject digital mediation entirely and maintain disciplined rhythms without technological aid. Their practice demonstrates that apps are not necessary. Yet this example does not negate the value of tools for others. It names a boundary. Necessity is not universality.

The reconciliation is practical wisdom. Tools are means, not measures. When means quietly become measures—when consistency is valued over attentiveness, streaks over presence—the practice shifts.

Streams and apps do not inevitably cause this shift. They invite it. Design nudges behaviour. Awareness resists drift.

This awareness deepens when we name what is at stake spiritually. Rhythms shape imagination. A practice entered through a notification may feel different from one entered through longing. Neither is pure. Both are human. The danger lies in forgetting which is which.

The bell as motif returns because it clarifies responsibility. A bell does not guarantee reverence. It marks time. The person must choose.

Digital bells are louder because they sit among other bells: emails, messages, alerts. Choosing which bell to heed becomes a moral act. The decision is concrete. Silence one. Attend to another.

Within this choice, agency can grow. Some practitioners deliberately reconfigure notifications so that spiritual reminders interrupt commercial ones. The visible behaviour is rearranged attention. The implication is subtle resistance.

No advice is needed to see the point.

As this section closes, the unresolved tension remains. If spiritual rhythms are increasingly mediated by systems designed for engagement, can regularity be gained without surrendering depth? Or does the very success of these tools demand a new discipline: not only of practice, but of choosing which bells we allow to ring, and when we let them fall silent?

Streaks, Badges, and Performed Piety

In June 2015, in Cupertino, Apple unveiled a set of coloured rings that would soon become ubiquitous. The Apple Watch's Activity Rings—Move, Exercise, Stand—promised a simple virtue: close the rings each day. Miss one, and the chain breaks. Within months, users spoke less about health and more about *streaks*. The rings did not measure virtue. They measured compliance. Yet they quickly acquired moral weight. To fail was to feel faintly at fault.

Metrics change motives.

The same year, religious apps began adopting similar mechanics. YouVersion's reading plans displayed consecutive days completed. Meditation platforms introduced badges for consistency. Prayer apps tracked minutes logged. None of this was hidden. The numbers were bright, friendly, encouraging. The concrete outcome was measurable: retention rose. Users returned. The cost was harder to name.

A paradox sits at the centre of this design. When devotion is tracked, does attention deepen—or does it perform? The datum is not mystical. It is behavioural. People optimise what is counted.

This question is not new. It is old enough to have been anticipated long before dashboards existed. In the first century, in Jerusalem and Galilee, Jesus warned against practising righteousness "to be seen by others" (Matthew 6). The concern was not hypocrisy alone. It was misdirected love. Acts meant for God were being bent towards an audience.

The image returns later in different traditions. Rabbinic writings caution against public displays that eclipse intention. Islamic scholarship distinguishes between sincere devotion and *riya*—acts done for show. Monastic rules warn against pride in ascetic feats. The names change. The pattern holds.

Show the mechanism and the modern parallel clarifies. Streaks and badges make devotion legible. They convert an inward practice into an outward signal. Name the effect and it sharpens: legibility invites comparison. Explain the implication and it unsettles: comparison reshapes motive.

Consider a second named example. In 2018, Duolingo, the language-learning platform founded in 2011 and headquartered in Pittsburgh, reported that streaks were among its most effective retention tools.

Users with active streaks were significantly more likely to return the next day, according to Duolingo's public blog posts that year. The metric worked. So did the pressure. Online forums filled with confessions of practising "just enough" to keep the streak alive.

Efficiency breeds shortcuts.

Translate this dynamic into spiritual practice and the risk appears. When the goal becomes maintaining a visible run of days, the content of the practice can thin. A hurried prayer replaces a slower one. A familiar passage is skimmed rather than wrestled with. The behaviour is visible: sessions shorten near midnight. The metric remains intact. The attention wavers.

This is not cynicism. It is design literacy.

A quiet motif helps carry the argument: the ledger. Ancient religions kept ledgers of a sort—days marked, fasts observed, psalms counted. But these ledgers were often private, or communal without being comparative. The modern ledger sits on a screen, bright and shareable. It invites an audience, even when none is explicitly present.

Trust becomes conditional.

Trust here is not belief in God or doctrine. It is trust in one's own practice. When a dashboard says "done," does the practitioner trust that something meaningful has occurred? The decision is concrete. Accept the badge. Or linger in silence without logging anything.

The counter-example matters. There are practitioners who use tracking tools without falling into performance. They treat streaks as scaffolding, not scorekeeping. Their behaviour shows flexibility: they break streaks without distress. They return without resentment. This limitation tempers alarmism.

Reconciliation lies in distinguishing *means* from *ends*. Streaks can support regularity. Badges can encourage beginners. The problem arises when encouragement becomes identity. "I am someone with a 300-day streak" is a subtle shift from "I am someone who prays."

Language reveals allegiance.

The comparison between a quiet, unmeasured prayer and a logged session clarifies the difference. The unmeasured prayer leaves no trace. No data point. No proof. Its value is relational, not archival. The logged session produces a record. It satisfies the system. The implication is not that one is pure and the other corrupt. It is that they form the heart differently.

Risk increases with visibility.

Risk here is measurable. Platforms that display leaderboards or social sharing amplify comparison. Even without explicit sharing, the internalised audience persists. Social psychologists have long noted that being observed—or believing oneself observed—changes behaviour. The famous Hawthorne studies in the 1920s showed productivity rising under observation, regardless of conditions. Observation mattered more than content.

Spiritual practice under constant measurement is always observed.

The ledger returns again. Once entries accumulate, they invite interpretation. A gap feels like failure. A long run feels like merit. Older traditions warned against this arithmetic of worth. Grace, in many theologies, resists calculation. The moment practice becomes currency, the economy shifts.

A further example sharpens the point. In 2020, during widespread lockdowns, several faith communities experimented with daily online challenges—prayer streaks, scripture quotas, fasting trackers. Participation surged initially, then dropped sharply. Interviews conducted by practical theologians in the UK and US noted a pattern: those who fell behind often disengaged entirely, citing shame rather than fatigue. The metric had become a gatekeeper.

Shame breaks rhythm.

This is the human cost of gamification when applied without discernment. The design intends motivation. The outcome can be exclusion. The implication is ethical, not technical.

Ancient cautions about performed piety were not anti-structure. They were pro-integrity. The issue was not public prayer, but prayer that needed an audience to exist. Digital badges can become that audience.

The motif threads once more. Ledgers can be audited. Hearts cannot.

As this section closes, the unresolved question remains deliberately sharp. If devotion is always visible—to ourselves, to systems, to imagined onlookers—what practices preserve secrecy, not as concealment, but as freedom? When the streak breaks, does the prayer break too? Or does something quieter, uncounted, continue beyond the reach of badges and rings, asking whether faith is being practised—or performed?

Creative Experiments in Depth

In April 2020, in the first weeks of lockdown, a Benedictine community in Collegeville, Minnesota, began streaming the Liturgy of the Hours from Saint John's Abbey. The monks did not optimise for reach. There were no graphics, no comment prompts, no calls to share. The camera remained fixed. The chant was slow. Attendance stabilised at a few hundred viewers a day. The concrete outcome surprised the organisers: messages arrived not asking for more content, but for *less*—requests to preserve silence, to resist pace. The date and place mattered. People were not merely bored. They were disoriented.

Depth had found a host.

A paradox follows. If digital platforms are engineered for speed and scale, how do practices that require slowness survive within them? The datum is simple. A livestream can carry a thousand voices at once. It can also carry a pause. The cost is not financial. It is intentional.

This section explores that cost through experiments that choose depth over distraction. Not despite technology, but by shaping it.

Show the experiment and the pattern emerges. During the pandemic, many communities attempted to reproduce existing rituals online. Some succeeded briefly, then faded. Others altered the form itself. Name the difference and it clarifies: replication versus translation. Explain the implication and it sharpens: translation demands constraint.

Constraint creates encounter.

Consider a second named example. In October 2021, in London, a small interfaith group launched an online retreat called *Stillpoint*. Attendance was capped at twelve participants. Sessions ran for ninety minutes on Zoom, once a week, for six weeks. Cameras stayed on. Microphones stayed muted during shared silence. There was no recording. The organisers published a brief report the following year noting retention above eighty per cent and unusually low attrition compared with larger online programmes. The metric was not clicks. It was continuity.

This was not nostalgia. It was design.

Abstraction often hides here. “Community” can mean anything. Pair it with behaviour and it becomes legible. Participants rearranged evenings. They declined other calls. They showed up on time. These are decisions. They signal value.

A quiet motif runs through these experiments: the circle. Not a feed. Not a stream. A circle implies faces, limits, return. Digital tools usually flatten circles into lists. These projects resisted that flattening.

Explain why this matters and the theological resonance appears. Many traditions understand encounter as reciprocal. One speaks.

One listens. Time thickens. Platforms tend to reward broadcast. Depth requires response.

The temptation is to romanticise scarcity. That would be an error. A credible counter-example tempers the claim. Large-scale digital gatherings can hold depth when designed carefully. In April 2022, the Jewish learning platform Sefaria hosted a global online *tikkun* for Shavuot, drawing tens of thousands across time zones. Sessions were varied, but several included extended text study with live annotation. Participation metrics showed sustained engagement beyond typical webinar drop-off points, according to Sefaria's published analytics that year. Scale did not automatically erase seriousness.

Reconciliation lies in recognising the variable that matters: agency. When participants choose how to engage, depth can survive. When engagement is pre-shaped for them, it thins.

Return to the circle.

The small, intentional online circle illustrates the core dynamic. Such circles often share features that seem minor but prove decisive. Fixed membership. Clear start and end times. Shared expectations about presence. These are not aesthetic choices. They are ethical ones. They answer a question that technology leaves open: *what kind of attention is required here?*

Attention is measurable. Cameras on versus off. Speaking turns honoured or overridden. Silence allowed to stretch without apology. Each behaviour encodes a value.

Name the risk and it becomes visible. The risk is not distraction alone. It is substitution—mistaking novelty for transformation. New liturgies proliferate online. Some refresh ancient forms. Others merely remix language over familiar rhythms of consumption. The difference shows up in retention patterns and post-event behaviour. Do participants linger? Do they return without prompts?

Metrics can serve discernment when used humbly.

The motif appears again. A circle can be drawn anywhere. It can also be broken easily. A notification interrupts. A tab opens. The experiment's fragility is part of its truth. Depth online is not guaranteed. It is practised.

Historical perspective steadies the claim. Religious creativity has always responded to new media. The codex altered scripture reading. The printing press reshaped devotion. Radio carried sermons into kitchens. Each shift provoked fears of dilution. Each also enabled renewal. The current moment differs not in kind, but in speed.

Speed tests intention.

Explain the implication for authority and formation and the argument deepens. When technology hosts genuine encounter, authority decentralises. It moves from the charismatic broadcaster to the shared practice. Collaborative projects—shared prayer documents, communal annotation of texts, co-written liturgies—redistribute authorship. Behaviourally, this looks like pauses while others type. Decisions to let a draft remain unfinished. Acceptance of ambiguity.

Ambiguity is not failure.

A further named case grounds the point. In 2019, before the pandemic, the Jesuit-run platform *Sacred Space*—founded in Ireland in 1999—introduced an experimental feature allowing small groups to pray through the daily reflection together online. Usage remained modest, but feedback highlighted a shift: participants described feeling "held accountable to silence," not content. The organisation's internal evaluation noted that the feature resisted easy scaling and therefore attracted less investment. Depth did not promise growth.

This is the structural tension. Platforms reward expansion. Depth often prefers fidelity.

The counter-pressure must be named. Not every community can sustain small circles. Access matters. Livestreamed rituals have lowered barriers for the housebound, the geographically isolated, the marginalised. To dismiss scale would be unjust. The reconciliation is not either–or. It is *both with clarity*. Communities can offer broad access while also cultivating spaces of greater demand.

Demand shapes practice.

The circle returns for a final time, not as nostalgia but as a diagnostic image. Does this digital practice gather people towards one another, or merely align them towards a screen? Does it ask something of them beyond attendance? These are observable questions. Attendance without alteration is one answer. Altered schedules, changed speech, sustained relationships are another.

As this section closes, the forward test remains unresolved by design. Technology can host genuine encounter. It can also host endless motion. The difference does not lie in the platform's capacity, but in the constraints communities choose to impose upon themselves. When digital creativity honours depth, it does so by narrowing the circle until faces reappear, silence is allowed to work, and the question quietly presses itself: how much structure are we willing to accept to make room for something that cannot be optimised?

Choosing Tools that Serve the Soul

On 25 May 2018, in Brussels and across the European Union, the General Data Protection Regulation (GDPR) began to apply in full. It arrived with the weight of law and the language of rights: data minimisation, consent, purpose limitation. For many people, GDPR surfaced as an irritation—new pop-ups, new boxes to tick. For others, it functioned as a moral jolt. It reminded ordinary citizens of a fact that had been easy to ignore: their lives were being recorded, analysed, and traded at scale. That realisation does not stop at shopping sites or social networks. It extends into the apparently gentler corners of digital life, including apps for prayer, meditation, scripture study, and spiritual direction.

Tools preach, even when silent.

Choosing spiritual technologies wisely begins with refusing a sentimental mistake: the belief that "religious" or "wellbeing" software is automatically benign. A prayer reminder is still a notification. A meditation app is still a business. A livestreamed service is still mediated by platforms with their own incentives. If the earlier sections traced how digital practice can be strengthened by scaffolding and then distorted by measurement, this final turn asks a simpler, sharper question. When you invite a tool into your inner life, what else have you invited with it?

The first answer lies in ownership. Ownership sounds abstract until it touches behaviour. Who owns the tool determines who can change it, monetise it, or sell it. A tool owned by a community organisation with transparent governance makes different choices from a venture-backed company obligated to grow. This is not a moral judgement against business; it is a recognition of incentives. A subscription model nudges one kind of design. Advertising nudges another. Donations nudge a third. The implication is practical: the business model becomes a spiritual environment.

A named example makes this concrete. YouVersion, launched by Life.Church in 2008 in the United States, is provided free and widely used, and it has built a vast ecosystem of reading plans and translations. It also collects usage data, like any large-scale digital service, to improve features and measure engagement. Many users experience it as a gift: scripture made accessible, habits made possible. Others worry about what "accessible" means when it includes analytics. Both responses can be reasonable. The point is to notice that spiritual practice has entered the world of product design, where "helpful" often means "sticky".

A second example sharpens the stakes around data. In 2018, Strava published a global "heatmap" of user activity that journalists and researchers noted could reveal sensitive patterns, including the outlines of military bases in conflict zones, because fitness tracking data was aggregated and visualised. The technology was not a prayer app, yet the lesson transfers neatly. Data that feels private in the moment can become public through aggregation, default settings, or future policy changes. When spiritual tools collect intimate information—prayer requests, journalling entries, confessional reflections, location-based routines—the potential sensitivity is higher, not lower. The risk is not melodrama. It is the ordinary consequence of databases.

Show the practice: a user logs a daily examen in an app, writing honestly about anger, desire, shame, hope. Name what is being created: an archive. Explain the mechanism: storage and synchronisation make retrieval convenient. Implication: what was once ephemeral and protected by forgetfulness becomes durable and portable, sometimes beyond the user's control.

This does not mean digital spiritual practice is reckless by nature. It means it requires the same seriousness we increasingly apply elsewhere. In older settings, certain spiritual acts were protected by architecture and custom. The confessional was a place; the prayer journal was a notebook in a drawer; the spiritual director was bound by trust. Digital practice dissolves the architecture. It relocates the act into systems designed for replication and memory. Wisdom asks what replaces the lost walls.

Design values matter as much as policy. A tool can have a strong privacy statement and still cultivate brittle souls by rewarding streaks, ranking users, or flooding them with prompts. Here, design values are visible as decisions: whether the app counts consecutive days; whether it emphasises silence or content; whether it encourages sharing; whether it uses social proof; whether it asks for permissions unrelated to core function. These are not technical details. They are moral cues.

A recurring motif can hold this together: the compass. A compass does not tell you where to go. It tells you where you are pointing. Spiritual tools, when chosen well, act like compasses. They orient attention towards what matters. When chosen poorly, they act like magnets. They pull attention towards what benefits the system.

This framing avoids two common errors. The first is fear: treating technology as inherently corrupting. The second is naïvety: treating technology as neutral. The more honest position is that tools are formative. They shape habits, and habits shape love. Therefore tool choice is not a side issue. It is part of spiritual discipline.

There is, however, a credible limitation that deserves respect. Many people will not read privacy policies, compare business models, or analyse design patterns. They are busy, tired, and trying to practise at all. The reconciliation is to make discernment simpler without making it shallow. You do not need to become a privacy lawyer or a product manager to choose more wisely. You need a small set of questions that cut through persuasion.

Begin with the question of *what the tool is for*. A tool that helps you keep a rhythm can be good; a tool that replaces the rhythm with performance can be corrosive. The behaviour to watch is how you feel when you miss a day. If missing produces shame that drives withdrawal, the tool has become a judge. If missing produces a gentle return, the tool remains an aid. The metric is emotional, not numerical.

Then ask what the tool *asks for*. If an app that offers daily silence requests access to contacts, precise location, microphone, and cross-app tracking, something has gone askew. If an app offers journalling but stores entries in a way that can be mined, shared, or retained indefinitely, the inner life has been treated as content. These are not accusations. They are signals.

Ask also what the tool *rewards*. Does it reward speed or depth? Quantity or presence? Does it make you feel hurried, or does it slow you down? Does it push you towards comparison, or does it cultivate privacy? Does it treat spirituality as a series of tasks completed, or as a relationship tended? Every reward structure is a theology in miniature.

A further question concerns *exit*. A wise tool allows you to leave without penalty. Can you export your data? Can you delete it? Can you continue the practice without the software? If you cannot, the tool has quietly positioned itself as necessary. Necessity is a strong claim. It should rarely be granted.

The compass motif returns here. A tool that makes itself indispensable does not merely guide. It governs.

None of this requires paranoia. It requires sober attention. The aim is not to achieve moral cleanliness by perfect purchasing decisions. It is to align means with ends. If a tradition teaches humility, then a tool that cultivates competitive streaks may be misaligned. If a tradition teaches secrecy in devotion, then a tool built around sharing and public progress may be misaligned. If a tradition prizes communal discernment, then a tool that isolates practice entirely may be misaligned. Alignment is not a slogan. It is a series of small decisions about what you repeatedly do.

At this point, a practical summary can be stated plainly, as a kind of internal checklist written in sentences rather than slogans. Before adopting a spiritual technology, name the practice it supports and the practice it might replace; check who owns it and how it makes money; notice what permissions it requests and whether they match its purpose; look for whether it tracks streaks, ranks behaviour, or invites sharing by default; ask what happens to your data if the company is sold, the policy changes, or the service closes; test whether you can delete and export what you create; observe your own motive after a week—do you feel drawn towards presence or towards completion; keep one practice deliberately untracked, so the soul remembers secrecy; choose one communal practice that involves other people's voices, so the tool does not become your only mirror; revisit the decision after a month, because the formation happens over time.

That is not legal advice. It is moral hygiene.

Notice what this summary does. It turns tool choice into an act of conscience rather than an act of consumption. It asks for periodic review rather than once-and-for-all certainty. It treats spiritual technology as a servant that can be dismissed, not as a master that must be obeyed.

The unresolved tension that ends the chapter remains the right one to carry forward. Digital tools can support sacred rhythms. They can also quietly train the heart to seek measurable reassurance. The decisive question is not whether the tool is clever, popular, or beautifully designed. It is whether it points your life towards what you claim to love—or whether, in the name of devotion, it teaches you to love the ledger instead.

Chapter 10
Designing Humane Systems

On a spring morning in March 2018, several engineers at Google gathered in offices across California and quietly declined to work on a project known internally as Maven. The project involved applying machine-learning tools to analyse drone footage for the United States Department of Defense. For some, the work was technically fascinating and legally permissible. For others, it crossed a moral line. Over the following weeks, thousands of employees signed a letter arguing that the company should not be in the business of building tools for warfare. By June, Google announced it would not renew the contract. The episode did not end debate about technology and ethics, but it revealed something crucial: systems are designed by people, and people can refuse.

That refusal did not come from a single prophet or a flawless policy. It emerged from conversations, pressure, conscience, and courage exercised within constraints. It was imperfect, contested, and costly. It was also human. The scene matters because it unsettles a common myth that has hovered over this book like a fog: that algorithms are forces of nature, and that those who live under them are merely weathered by their effects. The truth is stranger and more demanding. Algorithms are built, tuned, deployed, and defended through choices. Those choices can be argued with. Sometimes they can be changed.

Design is never neutral.

This final chapter turns deliberately from diagnosis to construction. The earlier chapters have traced how algorithmic systems shape belief, authority, conscience, and community, often in ways that feel inexorable. The risk of such analysis is paralysis: if the systems are vast and complex, what room is left for agency? The answer begins not with heroic redesigns or sweeping regulation, but with a shift in imagination. Humane systems are not defined only by what they optimise, but by what they *refuse* to do. They embody restraint as well as capability. They make room for uncertainty, dissent, and reversal.

They remember that power exercised without humility eventually corrodes trust.

The idea of humane design is not a novelty imported from spiritual reflection into engineering. It has deep precedents. In medicine, the principle of *primum non nocere*—first, do no harm—has long constrained innovation. In law, due process exists precisely to slow decisions that could otherwise be efficient but unjust. In religious traditions, sabbath laws interrupt productivity for the sake of life. Humane systems belong to this lineage. They are systems that accept limits, not because they cannot exceed them, but because they should not.

One way into this question is to consider transparency. Transparency is often invoked as a cure-all, but it is better understood as a discipline. To make a system transparent is not merely to publish documentation or release code. It is to allow those affected by decisions to see, in broad outline, how those decisions come about and where contestation is possible. An opt-in recommendation tool that explains why certain options are suggested, allows users to adjust the criteria, and can be audited by independent parties offers a glimpse of what this might look like. The visible behaviour is choice: the user can accept, modify, or reject the recommendation. The implication is dignity.

Humility follows close behind. A humble system does not claim omniscience. It signals uncertainty. It distinguishes between correlation and judgement. In practice, this might mean presenting confidence ranges rather than single scores, or offering explanations that admit limits. Weather forecasts have long done this, showing probabilities and cones of uncertainty. Their authority rests not on certainty, but on honesty. When systems that shape human lives—credit assessments, hiring tools, content moderation—speak with unwarranted confidence, they invite moral abdication. When they speak with measured restraint, they invite shared responsibility.

Reversibility may be the least glamorous principle, and the most humane. A reversible system allows decisions to be undone, appealed, or revised without disproportionate cost. In religious language, it leaves room for repentance. In civic language, it leaves room for appeal. In technical language, it resists lock-in. Consider the difference between a platform that permanently bans a user based on opaque criteria and one that offers graduated responses, clear explanations, and pathways to restoration. The first asserts control. The second exercises authority with care. Both moderate content. Only one treats persons as more than data points.

These principles—transparency, humility, reversibility—are not exhaustive, nor are they uniquely religious. What gives them their distinctive force in this context is the refusal to separate technical excellence from moral formation. They insist that how a system behaves teaches its users what kind of world they inhabit. A system that cannot be questioned trains passivity. A system that cannot be understood trains superstition. A system that cannot be escaped trains despair.

Responsibility for such systems does not belong to a single class of people. One of the more corrosive habits of modern life is the outsourcing of moral weight. Designers blame product managers. Product managers blame market demands. Institutions blame technology. Users blame institutions. Somewhere along this chain, accountability dissolves. The alternative is shared responsibility, which sounds abstract until it is grounded in practice.

At the intersection of technology and faith sit many kinds of practitioners: engineers who attend places of worship, clergy who manage livestreams, ethicists embedded in companies, community leaders choosing platforms for their congregations, and ordinary users deciding whether to click, share, or resist. None of these roles carries total control. Each carries influence. A small intervention at the right moment can change a trajectory. A team that insists on a pause before launching a feature that amplifies outrage may prevent harm that metrics alone would never register. A community that declines a tool because it violates its commitments sends a signal that values are not infinitely flexible.

A story of agency often begins quietly. A designer raises a question in a meeting. A leader asks whether a feature aligns with stated principles. A user opts out and explains why. These actions rarely make headlines. They do, however, accumulate. Culture is shaped less by grand declarations than by repeated refusals and careful yeses. In spiritual traditions, this is called formation. In systems design, it is called governance. The overlap is not accidental.

The horizon widens when institutions learn together. No single institution—legal, educational, technological, or spiritual—can address the formation of humane systems alone. The challenges are too entangled. Yet history offers encouragement. Previous media revolutions forced similar reckonings. The printing press disrupted religious authority, education, and politics in ways that were initially violent and chaotic. Over time, societies developed norms, institutions, and practices—schools, libraries, public debate, censorship regimes, reforms—that tempered its power without extinguishing it. The result was not harmony, but durability.

The analogy is not perfect, but it is instructive. Humane systems emerge when institutions recognise that they are co-learners rather than rivals. Joint charters that articulate shared commitments to dignity and accountability can shape expectations without prescribing technical detail. Learning spaces where engineers, theologians, lawyers, and educators speak across vocabularies can surface blind spots. Public rituals—graduations, commissions, blessings—can mark responsibility as a shared burden rather than a private calculation. These are not policy proposals. They are gestures towards a different posture.

What matters most is the direction of travel. A society that treats algorithmic systems as untouchable will eventually find its moral language shrinking. A society that treats them as tools subject to wisdom will argue constantly—and survive. The aim is not to freeze innovation, nor to baptise every new product. It is to cultivate a habit of asking, again and again, what kind of people we are becoming through what we build.

This returns us to the opening question of the book: when machines seem to know us better than we know ourselves, what happens to faith and freedom? The answer offered here is deliberately modest. Freedom is not preserved by ignorance, nor by domination, but by participation. Faith is not safeguarded by withdrawal, nor by uncritical adoption, but by discernment in practice. To design humane systems is to accept authorship without claiming control. It is to work with care in conditions of uncertainty.

The invitation at the close of this book is therefore not to agree with every argument, nor to master every technology. It is to make one small, specific commitment that resists fatalism. Commit to asking one more question in a meeting. Commit to choosing one tool differently. Commit to learning how a system that affects your community actually works. Commit to saying no, once, and seeing what happens. Such commitments will not save the world. They will, however, keep the future open.

That openness is not optimism. It is hope practised under constraint.

Principles for Humane Systems

In February 1975, scientists gathered at the Asilomar Conference Grounds in Pacific Grove, California, to decide whether they should slow their own work. Recombinant DNA research was accelerating, and its promise—medical breakthroughs, agricultural gains—sat alongside unease about unknown risks. Rather than wait for governments to intervene, the organisers, including Paul Berg of Stanford University, called a voluntary moratorium and convened peers to agree boundaries. The outcome was not prohibition but principle: containment standards, transparency, and ongoing review. Progress resumed, chastened and clearer-eyed. The scene remains instructive because it shows expertise restraining itself before harm demanded restraint.

The paradox lingers. How often do powerful systems pause themselves?

Five words suffice: *Build, then stop, then ask.* The cadence matters. The question at Asilomar was not whether knowledge should advance, but how responsibility should travel with capability. That question returns with force when algorithms shape attention, opportunity, and judgement at scale. The challenge now is not genetic material but informational power, and the stakes are social trust, moral agency, and the texture of everyday life.

This section shifts from critique to construction by asking what humane, spiritually literate systems might look like when built with intention rather than apology. The answer does not arrive as a blueprint. It arrives as a set of principles tested against practice, capable of guiding decisions when trade-offs press. Three principles recur because they address the deepest failures exposed earlier: transparency, humility, and reversibility. Each is ancient in spirit and modern in application. Each translates abstraction into behaviour.

Consider transparency first. Show. In October 2020, the Dutch government suspended its SyRI welfare fraud detection system after a court in The Hague ruled that the system violated human rights because citizens could not understand or contest how risk scores were generated. Name. Transparency failed. Explain. SyRI combined datasets to flag individuals for investigation without meaningful explanation or public audit. The implication was not merely procedural unfairness; it was fear, particularly among already vulnerable communities. Transparency, when absent, concentrates power and erodes legitimacy.

Transparency is not disclosure theatre. It is not a 60-page technical appendix no affected person can read. It is the practice of making reasons visible at the level decisions are felt. In visible behaviour, transparency appears as explanations users can interrogate, metrics they can contextualise, and pathways to challenge outcomes. A hiring tool that states which criteria weighed most heavily, allows candidates to request review, and publishes aggregate error rates makes its authority accountable. The metric is not perfection but contestability. The decision is not hidden; it is owned.

A limitation deserves air. Full transparency can expose systems to gaming or compromise intellectual property. Reconcile. Humane transparency is scoped. It reveals decision logic without surrendering security; it offers *why* without dumping *how*. Weather services manage this balance daily. They explain probabilities and uncertainties without publishing every line of code. Trust grows because candour replaces mystique.

Humility follows. Show. In May 2016, Microsoft released Tay, a conversational bot designed to learn from interactions on Twitter.

Within 24 hours, Tay had begun producing racist and inflammatory content. Microsoft took it offline. Name. Overconfidence. Explain. Tay was deployed with insufficient guardrails and an inflated belief in its capacity to learn safely from an adversarial environment. The implication was reputational damage and a lesson learned in public.

Humility in systems design begins with signalling limits. It prefers ranges to absolutes, warnings to bravado. The visible behaviour is restraint: confidence intervals displayed alongside predictions, labels that distinguish experimental features from mature ones, and documentation that states what a system cannot do. A medical triage tool that flags uncertainty and routes ambiguous cases to human review respects judgement rather than replacing it. The metric is escalation rate. The decision is deference.

Humility also reshapes language. Terms like "objective" and "neutral" recede, replaced by "trained on," "tested against," and "known limitations." This is not verbal hedging; it is ethical clarity. A credible counter-example arises when humility appears to slow progress. Reconcile. Progress slowed by humility is often progress redirected. Aviation safety improved not by denying fallibility but by designing for it—checklists, redundancies, black boxes. The result was fewer accidents, not fewer flights.

Reversibility completes the triad. Show. In March 2019, New Zealand's Accident Compensation Corporation paused an automated injury-claim triage tool after internal review raised concerns about bias. Claims reverted to human processing while criteria were reassessed. Name. Reversibility. Explain. The system was designed so decisions could be unwound without catastrophic cost. The implication was resilience: harm was limited because retreat was possible.

Reversibility treats decisions as provisional. It embeds appeal, review, and sunset clauses. The visible behaviour is a clear "undo": the ability to roll back updates, restore accounts, and re-evaluate scores. The metric is time-to-reversal. The decision is patience. When systems lack reversibility, errors harden into destinies. When reversibility exists, learning remains possible.

A credible limitation emerges: reversibility can be expensive and operationally complex. Reconcile. So is harm. Systems that cannot reverse often pay later through litigation, loss of trust, and regulatory clampdown. Reversibility is an investment in adaptability.

These principles converge in practice through concrete designs. Consider an opt-in recommendation tool for educational resources used by a professional association. Participation is voluntary. The system explains why resources are suggested, showing three factors—peer usage, topical relevance, and recency—each adjustable by the user. An independent auditor reviews aggregate outcomes annually, publishing bias assessments and error rates. Users can disable the tool at any time; recommendations disappear without penalty. The visible behaviour is choice. The metric is opt-in rate and opt-out ease. The decision is respect.

This example matters because it reframes authority. Recommendations guide without compelling. Auditability anchors trust. Opt-in resists coercion. The quiet motif threading this section is *the pause*. Each principle inserts a pause—before acceptance, before certainty, before permanence. Pauses are not inefficiencies; they are moral technologies.

The deeper claim is that humane systems are spiritually literate because they align with long-tested insights about human formation. Transparency mirrors confession: naming what is done and why. Humility echoes wisdom traditions that warn against hubris. Reversibility resembles repentance: the possibility of turning back. These parallels are not metaphors pasted onto code; they are structural resonances. Systems teach by what they require. When a system requires unquestioning compliance, it trains submission. When it invites understanding, it trains agency.

Pair abstraction with behaviour again. Trust appears when users continue to opt in after explanations. Efficiency appears when fewer escalations reach crisis. Risk appears as measured error rates rather than imagined fears. Each can be counted without being worshipped. Numbers serve judgement; they do not replace it.

The counter-example worth facing is the market incentive to optimise engagement at all costs. Systems built to maximise time-on-platform often resist transparency because friction reduces clicks. Reconcile. Humane systems redefine success metrics. They count long-term retention over short-term spikes, satisfaction over compulsion, repair over denial. This is not moral romanticism; it is strategic durability. Products that burn trust to grow quickly often plateau and fall. Those that cultivate trust compound quietly.

The Asilomar precedent returns here with force. The scientists did not abdicate responsibility to regulators. They authored constraints because they understood the cost of waiting. Designers and leaders today face a similar test. Will principles arrive after harm, or will harm be limited by principles? The answer is distributed. It lives in product reviews, governance boards, procurement choices, and user settings.

End with a test rather than a verdict. When a system you use explains itself, signals uncertainty, and allows reversal, does it feel weaker—or more trustworthy? When a system refuses to pause, what does it teach you about your role within it?

Shared Responsibility for Design

In June 2018, in Seattle and across Amazon's corporate offices, employees published an open letter asking their employer to stop selling facial recognition technology to government agencies. The product was Rekognition, and the letter argued that it could enable mass surveillance and disproportionate harm to marginalised communities. The outcome was not a neat corporate conversion, but it was not nothing: the protest pushed the issue into public view, catalysed external scrutiny, and helped set the stage for later decisions by several large technology companies to pause or restrict certain facial recognition sales in 2020. An internal document did not save the world. A collective refusal did change the conversation.

Responsibility spreads or disappears.

The myth this section confronts is seductive because it relieves anxiety: "Someone else will handle it." In technological life, "someone else" is usually imagined as a regulator, an ethics board, a product leader, or a distant class of experts with more time and cleaner hands. In religious life, the outsourcing instinct takes familiar forms too: "The leaders will discern." "The tradition will adapt." "God will provide." Each phrase can be true in a limited sense. Each can also become an alibi.

Five words matter here: *You are already participating, daily.* Participation is not only writing code or signing contracts. It is also adopting tools, accepting defaults, sharing content, tolerating harm, remaining silent in meetings, choosing convenience over care. Systems are built in design studios and server rooms, yes. They are also built in churches, mosques, synagogues, universities, council offices, family kitchens—wherever people decide what they will normalise.

Show the structure and the logic becomes plain. Modern algorithmic systems are socio-technical: the code acts, but it acts through institutions, incentives, and users. Name the consequence: there is no single author. Explain the implication: without shared responsibility, accountability evaporates. A scoring system denies someone a service and the story becomes fog. The vendor blames the client. The client blames procurement. Procurement blames compliance. Compliance blames the law. The law blames "innovation". Nobody sins. Somebody suffers.

Shared responsibility is not diffuse guilt. It is distributed agency.

Begin where agency is easiest to deny: the everyday user. Users like to imagine themselves powerless because it is emotionally simpler. Yet user behaviour is a measurable input into system dynamics. A platform that rewards outrage does so because outrage increases engagement. That is not a moral accusation; it is a behavioural fact. Time spent, links clicked, posts shared—these are quantifiable. The implication is uncomfortable: ordinary users co-train the environments they inhabit.

Still, it would be absurd to place equal weight on every actor. A teenager scrolling does not carry the same responsibility as a firm selling surveillance tools. Shared responsibility is not symmetrical. It is layered. Power creates heavier obligation. Yet even in layers, responsibility remains shared because influence travels in more than one direction. Users can migrate. They can refuse. They can demand. They can choose the slower option. Enough of those choices shift markets and norms.

Consider a second named example that clarifies how "small" interventions compound. In April 2021, Shopify, headquartered in Ottawa, publicly ended its relationship with a high-profile client (Kanye West's Yeezy) after backlash over product listings and content moderation controversies that intersected with hate speech concerns. The details were debated; the decision was not universally applauded. The point here is structural: platform decisions about who is allowed to trade, speak, or be amplified are exercises of moral governance at scale. A single policy interpretation becomes a cultural event.

Community leaders sit uncomfortably close to these decisions, even when they do not run platforms. A congregation choosing whether to host community discussion on WhatsApp, Facebook Groups, Discord, or a self-hosted forum is making a governance choice. The visible behaviour is where conversations happen. The metric is who participates and who leaves. The implication is formation: a community shaped by a platform's defaults will slowly adopt the platform's theology of attention, whether it intends to or not.

Designers and engineers, meanwhile, tend to narrate their work as problem-solving. That narrative is partly true and partly evasive. Problems are chosen. Success metrics are chosen. Trade-offs are chosen. A designer's most influential act is often not a flashy feature but a constraint: refusing to ship a mechanic that reliably increases engagement by increasing harm.

This is where a story of pushback matters. In September 2021, in Menlo Park, Facebook (now Meta) faced sustained criticism after the Wall Street Journal's "Facebook Files" reporting, which drew on internal documents and whistleblower Frances Haugen's disclosures. Among the claims aired publicly was that product teams repeatedly confronted evidence of harm—particularly around polarisation and teenage wellbeing—while struggling to prioritise mitigations against growth metrics. The outcome was not a single moral pivot, but it did produce hearings, reputational pressure, and internal re-evaluation of features and research access. The point is not to adjudicate every claim. The point is to see agency inside a machine: teams argued. Some pushed back. Some escalated. A whistleblower crossed a line of loyalty because conscience demanded it.

Agency is real.

Agency is also costly, which is why it matters that responsibility is shared. When only a lone dissenter is expected to resist, institutions grind them down. When dissent is normalised—through peer support, cross-functional review, external accountability, and leadership that treats pushback as a duty rather than disloyalty—humane design becomes more plausible.

Ethicists are often imagined as referees who appear at the end of development to deliver a verdict. That is a caricature. In practice, ethical guidance has impact when embedded early, close to decisions about data, objectives, and deployment contexts. Here, "ethicist" does not mean a philosopher in an ivory tower. It can mean a product manager trained to ask certain questions, a legal counsel who understands that compliance is not morality, or a community representative invited into design processes.

Pair every abstraction with a behaviour again. "Governance" looks like a pre-launch review that includes people affected by the tool. "Humility" looks like a feature postponed because uncertainty remains high. "Transparency" looks like an explanation interface that survives contact with non-technical users. "Reversibility" looks like an appeal mechanism that works without humiliation. Each of these can be measured: number of stakeholder consultations, rate of overturned decisions, time-to-reversal, percentage of users who understand explanations in testing.

These metrics do not replace virtue. They reveal whether virtue has been operationalised.

A credible limitation intrudes: shared responsibility can become a way of blaming everyone and therefore no one. Reconcile. The remedy is to pair shared responsibility with role-specific duties. The more power you have, the more you must do. A platform executive can change incentives and allocate resources. A designer can change defaults. A pastor can change community tool choices and language about technology. A user can change attention and consent. Shared does not mean vague. It means coordinated.

The quiet motif threading this section is the hinge. A hinge is small. It carries the door. Many interventions that change culture are hinge-sized: a default setting, a product requirement, a procurement clause, a community norm, a sermon that names a temptation without shaming, a classroom assignment that teaches students to read terms of service as moral texts. Hinges rarely look heroic. They simply keep the door moving in the right direction.

Risk, again, must be made concrete. Risk appears when decisions are made without accountability. It appears as error rates borne by the same communities repeatedly. It appears as time stolen, reputations damaged, opportunities denied. Shared responsibility insists that those costs are not "externalities". They are debts.

So where does this leave the intersection of technology and faith? Not with the fantasy that spiritual leaders will sanctify technology, nor with the opposite fantasy that engineers alone will save society through better code. It leaves us with a more demanding view of vocation: that each person is responsible for the part of the system they touch, and that their touch is never neutral.

The forward test at the end is simple, and it is meant to sting slightly. When you encounter a system that harms, do you ask who built it—or do you ask how you participate in it, and what hinge you might move?

Institutions that Learn Together

On 31 October 1517, in Wittenberg, Martin Luther sent a letter to Archbishop Albrecht of Mainz questioning the sale of indulgences.

Whether or not the Ninety-Five Theses were literally nailed to a church door, the documented outcome is clear: the printing press carried Luther's arguments across Europe within weeks. A technological shift collided with religious authority, legal power, and education systems almost overnight. Universities rewrote curricula. Princes rewrote laws. Churches split, adapted, resisted. The press did not *cause* the Reformation, but it forced institutions to learn in public, at speed, or be left behind.

Media revolutions expose institutional reflexes.

The analogy matters because algorithmic systems now exert a pressure similar in kind, if not in theology. Law, education, and spiritual life are being reshaped by tools that ignore institutional boundaries. Data flows across jurisdictions. Platforms educate outside classrooms. Moral formation happens in feeds long before sermons or syllabi intervene. When institutions respond alone, they fail predictably. When they learn together, something more resilient becomes possible.

The claim here is modest and demanding: no single institution can steward humane digital life on its own. Show the reality. Courts struggle to interpret opaque systems they did not design. Schools train students for a labour market already reorganised by automation. Faith communities grapple with moral questions framed by technologies they do not control. Name the pattern. Each institution sees part of the problem and overestimates its own competence. Explain the consequence. Gaps widen, trust erodes, and public life feels governed by forces nobody quite understands. The implication is collaboration, not merger—shared learning without collapsed identities.

Consider a first concrete example. In 2016, the UK's Royal Society and the British Academy jointly published *Data Management and Use: Governance in the 21st Century*. The collaboration mattered because it brought scientific, legal, and ethical perspectives into the same frame, rather than treating data as a purely technical or purely regulatory issue. The report did not legislate. It shifted language. Terms like "social licence" entered public discussion, signalling that legality alone was insufficient. The measurable outcome was influence: its framing informed subsequent parliamentary inquiries and educational debates. Direction, not detail, altered trajectories.

Educational institutions occupy a particularly exposed position. Universities and schools are both producers of knowledge and subjects of algorithmic assessment. Rankings, citation metrics, student satisfaction scores—these shape behaviour. Pair abstraction with behaviour. "Excellence" becomes publication volume. "Impact" becomes clicks. "Fairness" becomes standardisation. The risk is moral narrowing. Yet education also remains one of the few spaces where slow thinking can be defended institutionally.

Some universities have begun to treat digital ethics not as an elective but as a shared language. In 2019, the University of Helsinki launched *Elements of AI*, a free online course designed to give citizens basic literacy in artificial intelligence. By 2020, it had reached hundreds of thousands of learners across Europe. The point was not mastery. It was common ground. The implication for collaboration is clear: education can equip other institutions—courts, churches, councils—with vocabulary that makes joint discernment possible.

Spiritual institutions bring a different asset: long memory. They have navigated previous waves of technological and social change without disappearing, though not without wounds. When clocks became widespread in medieval Europe, monasteries were among the first to adopt strict timekeeping. Prayer hours were synchronised. Labour was disciplined. Time itself became moralised. The visible behaviour changed—bells rang, routines tightened. The implication was ambivalent: order deepened devotion for some and hollowed it for others. Institutions learned, slowly, that tools reshape souls.

That memory can temper present enthusiasm. When faith communities engage with digital systems alongside educators and lawyers, they contribute questions that resist reduction. What kind of person does this system assume? What kind does it produce? Where does mercy fit? These questions do not halt innovation. They complicate it, which is often what humane progress requires.

Legal institutions, for their part, specialise in boundary-setting. They translate moral intuition into enforceable limits. Yet law lags technology by design. This is not failure; it is caution. Courts rely on precedent. Legislatures rely on consensus. The danger arises when law is asked to compensate for absent cultural norms. A regulation written without educational understanding or moral imagination becomes brittle.

A credible limitation emerges here. Cross-institutional collaboration is slow. It risks dilution. Committees produce documents nobody reads. Reconcile. Collaboration need not mean permanent structures. It can mean periodic convergence around shared artefacts: charters, curricula, rituals, case studies. Learning together does not require agreement on ultimate meaning. It requires agreement on shared stakes.

The motif threading this section is the table. A table gathers different roles without erasing difference. Medieval guilds, early universities, synods, and courts all relied on tables—literal and metaphorical—as sites of negotiation. Digital life lacks tables. Platforms privilege streams, not gatherings. Institutions that learn together must therefore *build tables on purpose.*

What might those tables look like? Not policy minutiae, but directional practices. A joint charter between a city council, local universities, and faith organisations outlining principles for algorithmic procurement. A shared learning space where engineers present systems to non-technical audiences and answer unscripted questions. Public rituals—graduations, installations, civic commemorations—that name technological power explicitly and place it under moral scrutiny. Each is observable. Each can be evaluated by participation, continuity, and trust.

A second historical analogy sharpens the point. When radio emerged in the early twentieth century, institutions scrambled. In the UK, the British Broadcasting Company was formed in 1922, later becoming the BBC under a public charter in 1927. Its mandate—to inform, educate, and entertain—was a negotiated settlement between government, educators, cultural leaders, and moral guardians anxious about mass influence. The charter did not prevent propaganda or bias. It did establish a norm: broadcasting carried public obligation. The implication for algorithmic media is instructive. Norms precede enforcement.

Conflict will persist. Some institutions will prioritise innovation speed. Others will prioritise protection. That tension is not a bug. It is the learning edge. The danger is isolation. When institutions retreat into silos, each becomes caricatured by the others: law as obstruction, education as irrelevance, faith as nostalgia, technology as hubris. Learning together resists caricature by making disagreement concrete and accountable.

Efficiency must again be paired with decision. Collaborative processes take time. The metric is not speed but durability. Systems designed with cross-institutional input are more likely to survive scrutiny, adapt to failure, and retain legitimacy. That is not a moral claim alone; it is an empirical one, borne out in domains from environmental regulation to public health.

The forward tension that closes this section is unresolved by design. When a new system appears—scoring, surveillance, recommendation—do our institutions reach for separate statements, or do they reach for a table? The answer will quietly shape whose wisdom counts when innovation accelerates again.

Co-Authoring the Future with Care

On 15 May 2024, in Brussels, the European Council gave its final approval to the EU Artificial Intelligence Act, the world's first broad, horizontal law attempting to govern AI by risk category. The Act set out obligations for "high-risk" systems, restrictions on certain uses, and penalties for non-compliance. It did not solve the moral question of machine authority. It did, however, make one thing unmistakable: societies are beginning to write rules for algorithmic power in public, rather than treating it as a private affair of engineers and markets. A legal text cannot grant meaning, but it can draw lines.

Lines, of course, are not lives.

The opening of this book described a world of prediction meeting a world of prayer—dashboards and data streams brushing up against calling, grace, and freedom. That tension has travelled with us through stories of fate, the anatomy of black boxes, the personalised self, the seductions of probability, and the rearrangement of authority and community. If the chapters have done their work, you may now feel a particular kind of unease: not fear of machines as monsters, but unease at how easily human beings slip into spectatorship. We watch systems decide. We accept their suggestions. We complain about their harms as if they were storms. Then we call this realism.

It is not realism. It is abdication.

The central claim with which we close is both sobering and liberating: algorithmic life is not a destiny descending upon us; it is a set of choices accumulating around us. Show the accumulation and it becomes visible. A school adopts plagiarism detection software without debating its data practices. A hospital buys a triage tool and treats its outputs as impartial. A church livestreams services on a platform whose incentives warp attention. A family hands a child a device because everyone else has done so. Each decision is small. Each decision is legible. The implication is that fate, in an algorithmic age, is often just a story we tell about our own habits.

Five words can interrupt that story: *Someone chose this. So can you.* Short sentences matter because they can be remembered under pressure. The book has argued for literacy: understanding how systems predict, optimise, and shape behaviour. Literacy, however, is not enough. A society can be literate and still be compliant. Knowledge without agency becomes a new kind of fatalism, one that congratulates itself on being informed while remaining unchanged.

So the invitation is not to become a flawless resistor of technology. That would be another fantasy, and a tedious one. The invitation is to see yourself as a co-author rather than a spectator. Co-authorship sounds grand until it is grounded in practice, which is precisely why it matters. An author does not control every reader's interpretation. An author does not control every market force. An author does, however, choose words. An author edits. An author accepts responsibility for the sentences they release into the world.

Algorithmic systems are written in a similar way: not by a single pen, but by countless small inscriptions—defaults, metrics, incentives, procurement choices, community norms. When you participate in these inscriptions, you are already co-authoring. The only question is whether you do it awake.

At this point, the suspicion may arise that "co-authorship" merely relocates responsibility onto individuals and lets institutions off the hook. That would be a fair criticism if co-authorship were framed as self-help. It is not. Co-authorship is the opposite of atomised moral heroism. It assumes shared responsibility and differentiated power. Institutions must carry heavier obligations because they can do heavier harm. Yet individual actions still matter because they shape institutional incentives and norms. Consumers influence markets. Employees influence teams. Congregants influence churches. Students influence curricula. Voters influence law. Influence is not absolute, but it is real.

A second named, checkable example sharpens this point. In April 2018, residents of Toronto learned details of a proposed "smart city" development on the waterfront, planned by Sidewalk Labs, a company affiliated with Google. The project promised innovation—sensors, data-driven urban management—but it raised deep concerns about data governance and public accountability. After years of scrutiny, civic debate, and pushback from activists, scholars, and some public officials, Sidewalk Labs announced in May 2020 that it was abandoning the project, citing economic uncertainty. The outcome had multiple causes. The implication remains: when communities contest the terms of technological change, the future can be redirected.

Contest is a form of care.

Care is the proper word here because it prevents the closing movement from collapsing into either optimism or despair. Optimism is easy when one has not suffered. Despair is easy when one feels powerless. Care is harder. Care looks at harm without flinching and still commits to action. Care asks: what can be changed without lying about what cannot? Care does not demand certainty before moving. It demands honesty while moving.

Pair abstraction with visible behaviour again. Hope, in this frame, is not a mood. It is a practice. It appears as a meeting where someone asks for an audit rather than accepting a vendor's brochure. It appears as a community that chooses a slower platform because it aligns with its commitments. It appears as a manager who changes success metrics so that "time spent" stops being the supreme good. It appears as a teacher who includes algorithmic literacy in a curriculum without treating students as future technicians only. These behaviours can be measured: audit requests filed, defaults changed, time-on-platform reduced, error rates published, appeals honoured. The implication is that care becomes operational.

A credible limitation must be faced without melodrama. Many people do not have the privilege of opting out. Workers cannot always refuse surveillance tools. Citizens cannot always escape state systems. Students cannot always choose alternatives. Reconcile. Co-authorship does not require exit. It requires voice, solidarity, and targeted constraint. Where exit is impossible, the moral task shifts: build appeal mechanisms, insist on transparency, create support networks, document harm, pressure institutions, and cultivate habits that protect the interior life from becoming entirely quantified. Co-authorship in constrained conditions is not a romance. It is endurance with intention.

The motif threading this section is the pen. Not the pen as symbol of individual genius, but the pen as ordinary instrument: used, misplaced, found again, shared across a table. Pens do not command history, yet history is written with them. In an algorithmic age, the "pen" may be a setting, a policy clause, a procurement decision, a shared norm, a refusal to ship a feature, a demand for explanation, a conscious pause before clicking "accept". None of these will feel dramatic. Dramatic is not the point.

The final reflection therefore turns towards a small, specific commitment—not as a programme, but as a diagnostic. Name one system that shapes your life and ask a question that you can actually act on. What, exactly, does it measure? What, exactly, does it reward? Where, exactly, can I say no? If you are a designer, name one metric you will no longer treat as holy. If you are a leader, name one tool you will not adopt until it can be explained to those affected. If you are a teacher or parent, name one habit that protects attention from being wholly colonised. If you are a citizen, name one public decision where you will ask for accountability rather than accepting inevitability.

These commitments are not guarantees. They are openings.

The book began with a world of prediction meeting a world of prayer. It ends with the same collision, but with a different posture. The question is no longer whether algorithms will challenge belief—they already do, by shaping what we see, whom we trust, and what we call inevitable. The question is whether we will allow that challenge to reduce us to spectators, or whether we will answer with careful authorship: transparent, humble, reversible, shared. The future will be written either way. The only unresolved issue is whether you will recognise your own handwriting when you see it.

About the Author

Mira Qadari writes at the meeting point of faith, ethics, and technology, helping readers name what they feel but cannot yet articulate. Her work is shaped less by laboratories and boardrooms than by years spent listening to how ordinary people describe their encounters with code, institutions, and the sacred. She is interested in what happens to conscience, community, and hope when the language of risk and optimisation enters everyday life.

Raised between traditions that argued fiercely yet prayed side by side, Mira developed a habit of translating across worlds early on. She draws on the long history of religious engagement with new media, from handwritten manuscripts to broadcast radio and early television, to show that today's questions about algorithms and authority are part of a much older conversation about power and trust.

Beyond the page, she has collaborated with educators, community organisers, and technologists seeking wiser ways to use digital tools. She has also mentored younger readers and students learning to think critically about platforms without losing their sense of wonder. Mira brings those practical debates into her writing, offering readers clear frameworks rather than slogans. Her aim is simple but demanding: to help people live with integrity when machines have a great deal to say about what comes next.

www.ingramcontent.com/pod-product-compliance
Lightning Source LLC
Chambersburg PA
CBHW031347230926
51848CB00002B/420
* 9 7 8 9 3 7 5 3 6 1 4 3 5 *